Praise for *Neither*

"A chronicle extraordinary for its d
depths... This is a sobering, huml
one that every American should reau.

— *Yoga Journal*

"This is one of those rare works that once you've read it, you can never look at the world, or at people, the same way again. It is quiet and forceful and powerful."

— **American Indian College Fund**

Praise for *The Wolf at Twilight*

"Emotionally arresting... Nerburn shines when describing the humor and heartbreak he finds on South Dakota's Pine Ridge Indian Reservation.... Heartfelt wisdom is found throughout Dan's quest for closure and the tale is beautifully told."

— *Publishers Weekly*

"After my prison cell began to cool from the day's heat, I opened Kent Nerburn's creative and compassionate book, which I found humorous, hilarious, and at times very sad. Thank you, Kent, for a good book to read. Doksha."

— **Leonard Peltier**, author, artist, and activist

"Elegant, yet powerful... Nerburn crosses borders with a single-minded dedication to preserving an oral tradition. The emotional truth that resides in the rich storytelling is a testament to the strength and endurance of Lakota culture and... removes barriers to understanding our common humanity."

— **Winona LaDuke**, founder and executive director of the White Earth Land Recovery Project

"The story of this unique and captivating journey should be accepted with an open heart. It is a remarkable gift that we are honored to receive and obligated to pass on."

— **Steven R. Heape**, Cherokee Nation citizen
and producer of the award-winning documentary
The Trail of Tears: Cherokee Legacy

"Offers a sensitive, insightful glimpse into a Lakota soul, a feat unattainable by most non-Native writers."

— **Joseph Marshall III**, author of *The Lakota Way*
and *The Journey of Crazy Horse*

Praise for *The Girl Who Sang to the Buffalo*

"Simply riveting. Kent Nerburn has the very rare ability to gently and compassionately teach in a respectful way. I love this book. And so does the rest of our staff."

— **Susan White**, manager of Birchbark Books

"How do you live when you don't know what spirits to believe in? *The Girl Who Sang to the Buffalo* poses this question for Natives and non-Natives alike. In it, a mysterious Native American girl named Yellow Bird from an Indian boarding school shows us what we already know within ourselves about which spirits to follow. With this book, Kent Nerburn leads us on a search through old and new Native America in a touching and enlightening pursuit of spirit."

— **Chris Eyre**, director of *Smoke Signals*

VOICES
in the
STONES

Also by Kent Nerburn

Calm Surrender

Chief Joseph and the Flight of the Nez Perce

The Girl Who Sang to the Buffalo

A Haunting Reverence

Letters to My Son

Make Me an Instrument of Your Peace

Neither Wolf nor Dog

Ordinary Sacred

Road Angels

Simple Truths

Small Graces

The Wolf at Twilight

Edited by Kent Nerburn

The Wisdom of the Native Americans

The Soul of an Indian

Native American Wisdom

VOICES
in the
STONES

Life Lessons from the Native Way

KENT NERBURN

New World Library
Novato, California

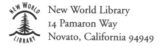 New World Library
14 Pamaron Way
Novato, California 94949

Copyright © 2016 by Kent Nerburn

All rights reserved. This book may not be reproduced in whole or in part, stored in a retrieval system, or transmitted in any form or by any means — electronic, mechanical, or other — without written permission from the publisher, except by a reviewer, who may quote brief passages in a review.

Some names and identifying characteristics have been changed to protect individuals' privacy.

Library of Congress Cataloging-in-Publication Data is available.

First printing, December 2016
ISBN 978-1-60868-390-1
Ebook ISBN 978-1-60868-391-8
Printed in Canada

 New World Library is proud to be a Gold Certified Environmentally Responsible Publisher. Publisher certification awarded by Green Press Initiative. www.greenpressinitiative.org

10   9   8   7   6   5   4   3   2   1

Quietly, for Raymond

❖

Do not begrudge the white man
his presence on this land.
Though he doesn't know it yet,
he has come here to learn from us.

— A SHOSHONE ELDER

⁘

CONTENTS

PREFACE

To MOST OF US, Native America is an unknown world shrouded in myth and misconception. To the extent we think of it at all, we imagine a world of drunks, welfare cheats, and casino millionaires or, conversely, elders possessed of deep, mystical earth wisdom.

What we don't see are people who predate us here on this continent and who, in their many ways and many centuries of life here, have evolved a way of understanding and interacting with the land that is at once distinctly different from the Euro-American way and rich with a knowledge of its own.

For almost three decades I have lived and worked among these people. What those years have shown me is that there is something fundamental in the Native way of seeing and living that has much to teach us all. It is something about being human, about living humbly on the earth.

Over the centuries and generations, all cultures develop and refine a particular genius. The genius of the Native peoples has always been to care for and pay deep attention to the relationships of nature.

They do not build, they listen.

They seek harmony, not mastery.

They value connections, not distinctions.

As one elder put it, "We are an honoring people, not a discovering people. We look upon life as a mystery to be honored, not a puzzle to be solved."

How far this is from our contemporary way of understanding, where our relentless and insatiable curiosity has allowed us to split the atom, cure disease, and advance the cause of human civilization in unimaginable ways, but has often left us bereft of humility in the face of our human limitations.

In my thirty years of friendship with Native peoples, I have tried to learn the lessons they have to teach. These lessons were often revealed obliquely, couched in metaphor or hidden from direct sight by years of cultural deterioration and transformation. Often, like tiny flowers unfamiliar to the untrained eye, they were hardly visible at all, and as easily overlooked by the outsider as they were taken for granted by those whose lives had been spent in their constant presence.

A mother speaking of her enigmatic son as impossible to understand without "looking at the landscape all around him" did not see this as a contemporary expression of the

Native way of learning by constant observation of the natural world.

A man speaking of a recently deceased relative as having "walked on" rather than having "passed away" did not see this as an example of the Native belief in death as part of a continuous journey in contrast to our more Christian idea of death as a disjunctive event that removes the dead from our presence.

To someone unfamiliar with the Native way of understanding, these moments might seem to reflect nothing more than choices of language or quirks of expression. But to those who know the Native people, these are but the shorthand references to a world of deeper meaning, a world that reveals itself every day in the most ordinary ways and in the lives of the most ordinary and unassuming people.

It is this world that I would like to share with you. And it seems only fitting that I should do it in the way that I was taught by an Ojibwe man who was counseling me on how to work with the children in his community.

"Always teach by stories," he told me. "People learn best by stories, because stories lodge deep in the heart."

Let us begin, then, with a story you should know, but may not have heard. It is the story of how the Native people see the world they now live in and how it came to be.

PROLOGUE

The Unseen Journey

Imagine an America without roads — a vast, borderless landscape of trails and mountains and forests and valleys and meadows and river bottoms.

Imagine a life where all settlement and movement are governed by the availability of water; where rivers are the most important thoroughfares.

Imagine a time when no human moves faster than a person on foot or, in the few cultures that have access to the horse, a person on horseback.

Imagine hundreds of groups of people with different languages and ways of life passing each other, trading with each other, interacting with each other, sometimes marrying each other, and sometimes fighting with each other.

All of this we can do.

But what we cannot do is imagine a world where the camas bulbs come out because we sing their song, or the raven sitting in the tree high above us might be bringing us a message; where the improbably shaped round rocks on the tops of mesas took their shape from looking at the moon and the sun; where the bear we see moving hump-backed across the meadow is endowed with special medicine powers that it can choose to share with us or withhold, and the coyote skulking on the edge of the clearing might be one of our enemies who has used his power to change his shape in order to observe our movements.

We cannot imagine this because we are simply too steeped in a world of rational principles to give ourselves over to a reality where everything — rocks, winds, animals, trees — is alive and speaking, if only we have the capacity to hear.

But let us go further.

Imagine a world where an uneasy feeling in the heart might be caused by the restless spirit of a body buried without proper ceremony in the ground where we are walking. Or a sickness in our stomach might be caused by someone far away who has managed to gain a lock of our hair. Or how in sleep we might be claimed by a dream and given knowledge we are bound to withhold or share. Or the calls of birds or the rippling waters of a creek might at any moment form into a song that contains a message or power.

It is, simply, a world where everything interacts and everything has power, and our modern rules of cause and effect don't apply; where plants have dominion, animals have dominion, trees have dominion — as do wind and water and clouds and spirits; where the dead are always present to guide us or afflict us, and neither time nor distance protects us from the power of our enemies.

Only right behavior and proper action can shield us from the forces that are swirling everywhere around us, and only respectful observance of the rules of life can assure us and those we love of a safe passage through this great intricate web of interconnected meaning.

But if we listen carefully, abide by the rules we have been taught, and learn the lessons from the world around us, we can align ourselves with those powers and use them for ourselves.

A mother, by feeding her child the eggs of the meadowlark, can claim the meadowlark's power of eloquent speech for that child. A boy or girl, just on the edge of puberty, can undertake a vision quest to meet a spirit guide — a person, an animal, a power of nature — that remains with them forever, to be called upon and commanded for use when needed in battle or to serve the good of the people.

A child on a vision quest who sees the morning star gains the power to foresee events; one who encounters the fish hawk can see into the body and cure illness; a sighting of a rock wren bestows the power to handle serpents; a child who sees a fog can control the weather.

With each of these powers goes responsibilities, and failure to meet those responsibilities or to show proper respect for what you have been given can result in that power turning on you.

Living in this great interconnected web of spirits whose powers cross the boundaries between species, and even the very line between the living and the dead, you learn to be less afraid of death than of a life poorly lived. At death you merely cross over into a different realm of the vibrant, interconnected universe.

But a life poorly lived can doom you and all your family to unimaginable misfortunes at the hands of those forces that you have insulted or shown disrespect, and those forces can follow you across the gossamer line between this world and the next.

So your task in life is not to dominate, but to understand; to learn the rules of the universe and come into right relationship with them. Then, and only then, will the Creator's favor be upon you and the powers of the world available and at your command.

Now, imagine that in a clearing or a field you are suddenly confronted by strange men of strange appearance and strange habits who have power far beyond any you have imagined — beings who have been granted the power of calling the sunlight into a piece of glass to bring forth fire; who have been shown medicines that can heal a man unable to walk, a woman unable to see, a child with a broken arm, a person with great sickness in the stomach.

How favored, then, would you believe these men to be, who have guns more powerful than the bows that had been shown to you by the Creator and cures more powerful than anything your medicine men possess?

With your openness to the world and your belief that all things have been placed on the earth by the Creator and that mastery over the earth reveals favor in the Creator's eyes, would you, too, not have seen these men as more than just another tribe, but perhaps as the bearers of a truth greater than any that had been shown you and any other people you had ever encountered?

·⁖·

Travel forward. The years progress. These new people have come among you in increasing numbers. They have brought skills, technologies, diseases, and ways of life that are strange and unsettling to you.

Most of all, they have brought claims of a different understanding of the Creator.

For you, the presence of the Creator — the Great Mystery — has never been in doubt. It lies at the heart of every aspect of life. It inhabits every tree, every stone, every creature, and every event.

Your elders have taught you the ways and ceremonies passed down from your ancestors and shown you how to live in humble awareness of the forces that pervade all of creation. But these new people, with their new power and new ways, have brought a different understanding of the Creator.

They claim a new truth — one that was not given to you — and a new understanding of what the Creator wants.

They tell you it is written in a book that only they have, and it has rules for life that carry dark sanctions if they are not followed.

It tells of a world you did not know, where after death you go either to be with the Creator or to a place of eternal fire where you burn without mercy for all time to come.

It tells of a god-man named Jesus who lived far away in a place unknown to you and whose life and death carry the key to leading you to the Creator or sending you to the place of endless fire.

This way is foreign to you. You are curious, but wary, and troubled by the fear it puts in your heart. Yet the powers of the new people speak of favor in the eyes of the Creator, so you cannot dismiss what they have to say.

These new people have a strange way of living, where all is divided into "mine" and "yours." They begin taking your land, telling you that you must leave the place where the Creator put you and change the way you live.

They do not understand your families, your way of sharing, your relationship to the Creator, your way of raising children and honoring the elders, or what constitutes the right conduct of life.

They cannot understand that silence before speaking is the sign of a composed and reflective mind, that interrupting another is an act of deepest disrespect, that children are to be raised in a certain way and elders are to be treated in a certain manner, and that the correct ceremonies must be performed to keep your life and the earth in balance.

They do not see the world as a place to be listened to and observed; where the dead are present to you at all times; where the powers of the animals, the trees, the rivers, the clouds can be granted or withheld; where everything is a message, everything is a lesson, everything is a story set down by the hand of the Creator, not to be used or abused, mastered or dominated, but to be understood and honored in the prescribed way.

You try to avoid these people or accommodate them, but your heart is troubled.

They are driving you from your homes, your way of living, your way of honoring the Creator. They take from you whatever they want and insist that their way should govern all your dealings with them. They do not use their language to speak from a pure and clear heart, but to twist the truth and get their own way.

·:::·

More years pass. These new people are everywhere. They are a people of demands, who understand nothing of giving but everything of taking.

Honor, respect, humility, and all the values taught you by your elders are of less importance to them than constant labor to acquire earthly goods and power.

They live for the future and have no concern for the past. Everything is about what they can become and what they can obtain, not about responsibility to the place from which they came.

They fear death more than they fear a life poorly lived, and they are interested in the land only for what it can give to them rather than for how it speaks to them.

By sheer force of numbers these new people have begun to impose their will on you. They make you move from your homes, they put a price on everything, they build their lives around ownership and make agreements they do not keep.

They care little about your ways, but insist that you follow theirs. Their earthly skills and power seem to overwhelm your traditional ways and power.

Little by little, your world is fracturing.

Your young men begin to berate the old men and call them cowards for not resisting these newcomers; your old men berate the young men for naively thinking that they can resist the force of these people who are becoming as many as the stars in the sky.

Some among you decide to live as the newcomers do; others try to keep to the old ways. There are days when it seems like the Creator has withdrawn all favor from you and left you without guidance and power upon the earth.

No one knows what to do. The newcomers have taken your land. They have taken your homes. They have taken your food and your god and your way of life.

Then the day comes when they decide to take your children.

They set up schools run by their government and their churches and tell you that you must send your children to them. If you resist, they will take your children by force or punish you by withholding food and the goods you need to live.

Your children are put on trains and in wagons and taken to these schools, where their hair is cut, their heads washed in kerosene, and they are made to burn the clothes their grandmothers made for them and forced to wear uniforms of the newcomers' ways.

They are made to eat strange food and are not allowed to speak their own language. They are disciplined by beatings and imprisonment in small dark rooms.

In the worst of these places they are tortured and abused.

They are taught to hate who they are and to believe that their parents and grandparents are going to go to the place of eternal fire because of what they believe and how they live.

They are raised without love and are filled with fear. They are never held and hugged. Their only human touch is by the strap or the fist.

They are raised with rules and punishment, not with visions of who they should be.

They are taught to live for themselves and to forget their people.

They are told not to listen to the grandmas and grandpas and uncles and aunts, because their ways are the ways of evil; to forget service to the people; and to concern themselves with following the rules that will keep them from the place of fire.

They learn only the skills that will allow them to live in the newcomers' world.

Through beatings, teachings, isolation, and fear they are made to turn against the ways of the ancestors and accept the strange, selfish ways of the newcomers.

Back in your homes you live in mourning.

Your communities are shattered. Your men can no longer provide for their families and are filled with shame. The grandmas and grandpas have no children to teach. The mothers see their children taken from them and raised in schools governed by the harshness of men rather than the love of women.

The older youth, returned from these schools, have no work and none of the old skills. They do not trust the past, and they have no hope for the future. They use alcohol to numb their memories and fill their days. They understand more of physical violence than they do of love. You no longer even know who they are.

Sickness, of both the body and the spirit, is everywhere.

The newcomers who have taken over the land have broken every promise they have made to you and treat you like children.

They had promised you would be equal to them and they would speak to you as people to people.

Now they have placed a government over you that tells you how you must live and keeps the money they owe you for what they have taken from you, telling you how it must be spent and making you beg for what is rightfully yours.

You practice the old ceremonies in hiding so you are not subject to punishment, but they seem to be without power. You teach the old ways to the children when you can, but the old ways do not feel full, as they did before. Your children have been deprived of their language, where the connection to the spirits lay, and now speak only the English of the newcomers. The world has become a hollow place of hopelessness and memories.

❖

More years go by. You now live unnoticed in the cities of the newcomers or on small pieces of land that they have allowed you to keep.

Your people are almost forgotten in this new world.

The land is so full of these newcomers, and their ways are so entrenched, that the land almost seems not to know you. You are but a remnant in a place that was once the Creator's gift to you.

Other people from other places have come to this land that the newcomers call America, some coming with hope, some brought against their will, all filling up the land that was once yours.

Because of their skin color or their language or the land of their birth, these new arrivals have been denied the power and ownership the first newcomers claimed, and now they want to share in them.

You feel sympathy for these new arrivals, but their experience is not yours.

You are the ones who were here first, before any of the others arrived — you are the invaded ones, the ones who see through the eyes of a conquered, betrayed people. You wish only to protect what little you have left, to be able to control your own lives, and to find such connection as you can with the land and ways of life that were yours before the newcomers arrived so many years ago.

More than wanting to share in the newcomers' world, you wish to be left alone.

You try to be heard, but this new America does not choose to listen to you. You are invisible. They group you with the others who have been denied their rights and pretend they can make things right by granting you those rights.

They cannot accept that what has been done to you cannot be undone, that there is blood on the ground where they have walked and a wound in your heart that cannot be healed.

Instead of seeing you and hearing you and learning from you, they ignore you, treat you like children, or mythologize or demonize you, making you into wise men and earth mothers or layabouts and drunks.

They traffic in what they want you to be, claiming the most private and sacred of your ceremonies and selling their empty versions of your spiritual practices for profit. They reduce you to cartoons and caricatures and ignore the pain it causes you and your children.

They offer you an America you do not want, make you beg for what is rightfully yours, and speak of the small pieces of land on which you live as if they are gifts they have granted to you.

They fill you with anger and shame and sadness.

The values taught by your ancestors, the values you were taught to live by, the values in which you believe — humility, service, compassion and kindness toward the weak, generosity, reserve, and a sense of personal decorum — have no place in this new land where everyone seeks to rise above every other and the weak are left at the mercy of the strong. You and the truths of your ways are forgotten in your own land.

Your grief runs to your very core. You cannot live in the old way; you do not wish to live in the new.

Generations of broken families and broken hearts, physical abuse in the boarding schools, shame for your traditional beliefs, and the loss of your ways of raising children, shaping a family, supporting your loved ones, and honoring the elders, have damaged you almost beyond repair.

You survive in a wreckage of abuse and alcohol.

The ghosts of the old ways still speak, but their voice is fading. In your heart and in your world, they have almost ceased to exist.

❖

Come forward to today.

You see the ways of the newcomers beginning to fail. Their faith in the future has caused them to ignore the lessons of the past. Their belief in the individual has caused them to lose touch with the ways of the Creator.

Their concern with the human has deafened them to the voices of the other creatures and of the very earth itself. Their love of freedom has made them blind to responsibility.

The memory of your ancestors and the ways you were taught have kept you strong, though wounded.

You know that the way of power and ownership, of "mine" and "yours," is not a good way to live. It is a way of domination, and domination does not care for the weak or give voice to the voiceless.

It seeks not to serve, but to be served.

It causes life to be out of balance.

You sense a growing confusion in the newcomers, who now are in almost full possession of the land that was once yours.

They, too, hear the distant voices, the voices that spoke through your ancestors, but they do not know what they are hearing.

They have a hunger that has no source, they seek a justice and a balance that they cannot understand.

You know that justice and balance are in the ways of the old ones, in the ways of listening and honoring and sharing, not in the empty notions of freedom and ownership that are at the core of their understanding of life.

You know that the newcomers are good people, who, like you, love their children and wish to live in a world of peace and kindness. But their way, the way that runs so deep in their understanding, has betrayed them. It has caused them to act in ways that stand against the laws of creation.

You wish to help them and guide them, to share the lessons the elders taught you. But you were trained to speak softly and to offer counsel only when it is sought. And they do not seek your counsel, because they see only the wreckage of your lives or the illusions of who they imagine you to be.

You ask the Creator for the wisdom and patience to wait. You look to the ancestors, who told you to hold fast to the old ways. You try to keep the fires of the old beliefs burning in your hearts.

But in the deepest place in your spirit, the place of wounds and hope, you know that the earth is speaking, and that the time has come to listen to all of her voices.

You can only hope that for the sake of your children, and all the children of the world, that your voices, so long silenced and ignored, will be among those that are heard.

For that time, you and all the children of the earth are waiting.

-:::-

Such was the world I walked into on a warm day in September 1988 when I took a job in the deep pine forests of northern Minnesota on the Red Lake Ojibwe reservation, far from the large cities of America and the chatter and clutter of my traditional American ways.

The people looked the same as I did, dressed the same as I did, and in most ways acted the same as I did.

But their hearts were different; their minds were different.

They understood the value of words differently, the power of silence differently.

They watched me with careful eyes.

I had been hired to teach their children, and though my heart was earnest and my intentions were good, these people had been harmed by good intentions before. If I was to be a teacher, I needed to be taught. The lives of the children depended on it.

And so I became the learner.

Over the next three decades, in Red Lake and other places — from the lyrical, rolling hill country of South Dakota to the mountains of eastern Oregon and the windswept plains of Montana — that learning continued, and it continues to this day.

It runs deep, to the very core of what it means to be human.

In some ways it is simple — practices and values that illuminate another way to live. In other ways, it plumbs places that defy description and explanation and speaks to another reality that lives somewhere far beneath the practical and rational, like a sound not quite heard or a presence felt in an empty room.

Come with me now, and I will show it to you as best I can.

You have heard their story.

Now let me tell you some of mine.

1. The Native Way of Living

There were ideals and practices in the life
of my ancestors that have not been improved upon
by the present-day civilization.

— LUTHER STANDING BEAR

When you arise in the morning, give thanks for
the morning light. Give thanks for your life and strength.
Give thanks for your food, and give thanks for the joy
of living. And if perchance you see no reason
for giving thanks, rest assured the fault is in yourself.

— OHIYESA

WELCOME HOME

All People Must Find Their Own Spiritual Path

You should say nothing against our religion,
for we say nothing against yours.…We both pray
to only one God who made us all.

— SITTING BULL

"COME IN, NERBURN. Come in," he said.

His welcoming manner immediately put me at ease.

I was new on the reservation and had been given his name as an elder who knew a great deal about Ojibwe history. I had decided to visit him in person and ask if he would be willing to share his life stories with the students.

After a long drive through muskeg bogs and tamarack forests, I had arrived at his tidy clapboard home set far back in a wide field near the western boundary of the reservation.

He was a kind man in his mid-eighties who had been raised by grandparents who spoke no English. He moved slowly and deliberately and had a sanguine expression that never varied.

After greeting me with a soft handshake, he beckoned me to a table where he had laid out old photos of his family members and memorabilia from his grandfather's time fighting the Dakota.

"He was hit by an arrow and dragged all the way back here on a horse-drawn travois," he said. "He was a good man, my grandfather."

While he was speaking, he took out a piece of soft blanket and carefully unwrapped his ceremonial pipe. It was kept in two pieces — a red pipestone bowl and a long wooden stem.

He fit the bowl onto the stem, filled the bowl with a mixture of tobacco and dried willow bark, and very carefully lit it with a coal from his woodstove.

He drew long on it, puffing more than inhaling, until the air around his head was filled with a rich, aromatic scent.

He cupped his hand in the smoke and pulled it around his head, as if bathing himself in it. Then he rotated the pipe, stem out, in a clockwise direction, until it completed a full circle, and handed it across to me.

"Here. Now you," he said.

I was hesitant. I had only been on the reservation a short time and was not familiar with proper protocol. Even in the best of circumstances, I am not comfortable stepping into another's ceremonies, even when asked. Perhaps it comes from being raised in a Catholic tradition where you must earn the right to be part of the sacred rituals through long training. Facile participation in another's ceremonies — whether Christian, Native, or any other — feels to me like lack of respect for the deep spiritual realities of that tradition.

Still, my host had asked me to smoke, and, as the pipe had been extended to me, I had no choice but to accept. It was being offered to me as a gift, and in Native cultures, as in all traditional cultures, to refuse a gift is to refuse the offering of a person's heart. To refuse it would have been an insult.

With my eyes cast down, I took the pipe carefully, trying not to seem artificially pious.

I nodded slightly and cradled the long wooden stem in my hands.

The elder reached over and lit the bowl with another coal. I drew in the tobacco mixture and cupped the smoke around my head as I had seen him do.

I was not sure about the meaning of the ritual or whether I was performing it properly. But I did the best I could, rotating the pipe clockwise in a full circle and passing it back to my host.

The elder nodded to me and gave me a quiet smile.

I found myself swelling with pride, as if I had been allowed inside something private and sacred.

My response surprised me.

Even on those rare occasions when I had allowed myself to participate in the religious rituals and ceremonies of others, my overwhelming feeling had always been one of remaining comfortably outside, keeping my distance not only from the practices but from the heartbeat of the belief as well.

Their world was not mine, and I had no desire to make it mine. I was simply honoring their practices and feeling privileged to be witness to their spiritual ways.

But this time I had felt something different. I was like a child being granted entry to a place I dearly wanted to be.

Why, I wondered, did this feel so right, and why did it matter so much? The answer revealed itself slowly over my time among the Native people.

In the culture where I was raised, religion is generally understood as doctrine, not as a cast of mind.

Those who feel a strong sense of a spiritual presence in life, but do not adopt a recognized set of beliefs are somehow considered suspect. Their spirituality is seen as untethered, self-referential, and lacking rigor, and they are left homeless in a spiritual diaspora of their own creation.

There are many reasons why good, caring, spiritually inclined people find themselves in this situation.

Some are disaffected, alienated by a tradition that was forced upon them in childhood.

Others may feel that embracing a single doctrinal way negates all other paths, and they do not wish to be part of an exclusionary faith.

Still others may simply not have found a tradition that fits the shape of their spiritual hunger.

But whatever the reason, they find themselves outside of traditionally defined religious structures, yet feel a deep spiritual yearning in their hearts.

The Native way embraces this yearning — even honors it.

As Ohiyesa, the great Dakota teacher and thinker, said, "Each soul must meet the morning sun, the new sweet earth, and the Great Silence alone."

There is no need to justify the purity or sufficiency of your spiritual convictions, no need to defend them through theology or philosophy or argumentation. All that is necessary is that you acknowledge the Great Mystery that is behind everything and present in everything.

The Seneca chief Red Jacket put it succinctly: "We never quarrel about religion," he said, "because it is a matter that concerns each man and the Great Spirit."

This is what the old man was telling me as he reached the pipe across to me with his calm and welcoming smile.

I was not being asked to accept a particular belief or espouse a particular doctrine. I was being called to spiritual mindfulness, to recognize the spiritual in all creation, and to acknowledge that we were sitting together in the shared presence of the Great Mystery.

How I understood that Great Mystery and how I chose to worship it, if I chose to worship it at all, was between me and the Creator.

As I handed the pipe back to my host, I was overwhelmed by a profound sense of peace and well-being.

What more affirming experience, I thought, could there be than to be invited to enter a place where spirit, like the smoke, is everywhere, but ideology is nowhere?

It was more than an invitation to participate in a ritual not my own; it was a spiritual embrace.

And far from making me feel like a spiritual stranger, it made me feel, in a very deep way, that I was being welcomed home.

THE FEAST

Honor the Young and the Old, for They Are Closest to the Creator

The grandparents are old and wise. They have lived
and achieved. They are dedicated to the service of the young
as their teachers and advisers, and the young in turn regard
them with love and reverence. In them the Indian
recognizes the natural and truest teacher of the child.

— OHIYESA

The grandfathers and grandmothers are in the children.
Teach them well.

— OJIBWE SONG

EARLY IN MY TIME ON THE RESERVATION, I was asked to
attend a feast at the school where I was working.

I had no idea what a feast was. It sounded regal and
baronial, conjuring up images of Henry VIII at a great
plank table, or primitive and dangerous, with people danc-
ing ecstatically around a fire while eating the half-cooked
shanks of wild animals.

It proved to be neither. It was a simple, festive potluck gathering held in the school cafeteria in honor of a young boy who had received an award for a poem he had written. He was being raised up before the community and praised for his accomplishments.

It was much like any gathering in any community, but with one subtle but important difference.

In Indian country, the sharing of food carries spiritual significance because it is an act of generosity, and generosity is among the most sacred Native values. It harks back to the time in the Native past when a successful harvest or hunt was a cause for sharing and celebration.

When food was scarce, all went hungry.

When food was abundant, all ate their fill. ·

Those who had food to give considered it their sacred duty to see that others, especially the children and the elders, were properly fed. This practice of the sharing of food as a spiritual act has carried down through the generations and become the center of any celebration or gathering anywhere in Indian country.

I was standing at the rear of the room with Joe, a man about my age. He had returned to the reservation after years of living in a big city because he wanted to be immersed in his traditional culture and to raise his children in a more traditional way. He wore his hair in braids and had the soft-spoken, gentle manner I was coming to recognize as a characteristic of many traditional Native men. He and I were quickly becoming friends.

"See those girls?" he said, gesturing to a small group of girls about eight or nine years of age. "The one in the purple, she's my daughter."

The girls were gathered together in a far corner of the room. They stood quietly as an honoring song was played and the community spiritual leader said a long prayer in Ojibwe.

When the prayer was finished, the women who were overseeing the serving of the food peeled back the tinfoil covers on the large pans of venison stew and trays of wild rice and fry bread, and beckoned people to come forward.

Potato chips, brownies, casseroles, plates of sliced meat, and all manner of store-bought cookies and sweets were spread out on folding tables that stretched along the back wall of the room.

As at all gatherings in Native country, people of every age were present, from infants in their parents' arms to the elderly in wheelchairs.

At the signal that the meal was to begin, the children in attendance, ever anxious to eat, rushed to be first to the tables and stacked their paper plates and bowls high with the bounty laid out before them. The women who were serving the food smiled at them and guided them, sometimes reminding them not to take too much or to do less jostling and to be more patient.

The group of girls with my friend's daughter, however, held back. They were quiet, even reserved.

After the other children had jostled their way through the line and the adults were getting up to move toward the food, the girls approached the tables. Each picked up a paper plate and some plastic utensils.

They moved slowly down the food line, holding the plates up to the serving women who carefully ladled stew and potatoes and green beans and pieces of venison onto each of them.

The girls then carried the plates over to a group of elderly men and women who were sitting in the back of the room in wheelchairs and metal folding chairs.

Each of the girls handed a plate to an elder, who smiled warmly and took it with unsteady hands. The girls smiled in return and shyly averted their eyes.

Short conversations took place. Then each girl went back and filled a Styrofoam cup with coffee or water or Kool Aid or whatever the elder had requested.

They brought the drinks to the elders, then quietly went to the end of the line to wait for the chance to get food for themselves. No one paid them any mind or gave them any particular acknowledgment; they had merely been doing what was expected of them.

"That's the way it should be," my friend said. "The elders eat first, and the young people serve. This was the way we were taught, but we're forgetting the old ways."

There was a wistful yearning in his voice.

"The elders are sacred," he continued. "They have lived long lives, and their days have been hard. They've earned the right to be served because they've lived their lives serving others. Now the others should be serving them."

Across the room I could see the elders happily eating their food and laughing among themselves. The girls were watching closely to see if there was anything else they needed.

"It's good for the kids, too," Joe said. "It teaches them about patience and kindness and putting others before themselves. And it brings them close to the elders, who only want to give them love. If the kids aren't brought close to the elders, they end up being afraid of them. The elders seem so old. The kids see the ghost of something frightening in them.

"But if they're brought to the elders, they see that the elders' hearts are open wide to them. They're the farthest apart in years, but closest in their nearness to the Creator."

"You're a good teacher," I said. "Thanks."

"I'm just trying to school you a bit," he smiled.

Joe took his leave from me and walked over to talk with a man in a worn satin logging-company jacket. The two of them stood, laughing and joking together, sharing the easy camaraderie of old friends.

The feeling of common community was everywhere in the room. I kept thinking of the way Joe had spoken the word "elders" with such ease and grace. It was a word filled with gravity and respect; an elder was a status to be revered, not a simple condition of age.

Joe's daughter and her friends had gotten their food and were sitting together at a table on the far side of the room.

Joe made his way back to my side and gestured in their direction. "This is why I came back to the rez," he said. "In the city, among the white folks, the elders weren't even noticed. The kids only went to see them because they had to or because it was part of some school project. The elders weren't seen as teachers. They weren't seen as a chance to learn about life."

One of the girls had gotten up to help a woman in a long print dress refill her coffee cup.

"I remember when I was just a little guy my dad used to tell me that I needed to listen to my grandma and grandpa when they talked. He said they had walked the road I was going to walk and that their words could guide my footsteps."

"Did it work?" I asked, half joking.

"Pretty much," he said. "When Grandma gave me the

hard eye, I knew I'd better get back in line. You didn't mess with the grandmas."

He laughed self-consciously and put his hand on my shoulder.

"Come on," he said, pointing to the almost empty food line. "That's enough philosophy. It's time to eat. You know, if these were war times, we would have eaten first, because we would have needed to be strong to defend the camp and go out on hunts. But I don't see any wars on the horizon, at least not any we need to fight today. So we eat last. We'd better get up there now before the little rug rats rush up and take everything that's left."

We took our place behind the man in the logging jacket and a woman in a faded sweatshirt.

We patiently waited our turn — two men, neither young impressionable youths nor honored elders, but men in the middle, at the greatest point of our physical strength, but still only partly formed on our spiritual journey.

Across the room we could see the elders, smiling and laughing with each other and enjoying the activity and company of the community around them.

The young girls had finished eating and were taking the plates and cups from the elders. It was almost a visceral experience to see the fresh soft hands of the girls, so delicate and unformed, touching the twisted, shaking hands of the elders, whose long lives were written in every bent finger and scarred knuckle.

Joe's daughter said her good-bye to the elder she had served, then came over and pressed herself against her father, as if looking for his approval. He smiled and ran his hand gently through her hair.

"You did right, my girl," he said.

There was nothing else he needed to say.

···

In the world where I was raised, life has only a brief moment of flowering — the time of physical strength for men, the season of youthful beauty and childbearing for women. All else is a time of becoming or a time of decline.

Rather than looking at our lives like the seasons, where each has a richness that belongs to no other, we look at them like a flower that moves from bud to bloom to gradual decay and death. Only the time of bloom is seen as the fullness of life.

Native people like Joe do not see life this way. They see it as a passage through spiritual seasons where we gain knowledge and richness as we pass from one season to the next.

Only a person in winter has seen them all, so only a person in winter is granted the respect that comes with full spiritual knowledge.

Far from being vestigial or in eclipse, the elders, who have lived through all of life's seasons, are the honored ones, the crown jewels of the Native family.

At powwows they are given a place of honor. Before any speech or presentation, their presence is always acknowledged.

More than once, when I asked a student to do something with me or to perform a particular task, the student responded, "I have to ask my grandma."

I was reminded of one encounter that I had in our small town, thirty miles south of the reservation. It was only a small moment, but it spoke volumes about the significance of the elders to the Native people.

My stepson had ridden to town on his bicycle. He was young — no more than ten — and struggled to make friends.

On this Saturday morning he had left early, hoping to meet someone from school or to find something to fill his life with a bit of childhood adventure. So, when after only an hour he appeared at the door with a gloomy look on his face, I knew something bad had happened.

"What's wrong?" I asked.

He looked at me with a dark expression.

"Some Indian kid stole my bike," he said.

Our town, though surrounded on three sides by large reservations, was a bastion of white small-town culture built on its heritage as a lumber center in the early twentieth century. There were many Native families, and though we all brushed shoulders, our interaction was superficial.

The towns in the nearby reservations, small and ragged though they were, were "their" towns, and this was "our" town — the "white" town. The Native folks stayed mostly in the background and kept to themselves.

My stepson's encounter was in no way out of the ordinary. To be sure, it had a racial component to it, but mostly it was just the typical rough-and-tumble interaction of preteen boys.

Still, one of these boys had stolen his bike. I needed to get involved.

So we got in the car and drove to the scene of the theft. Three or four young Native boys were riding around on dirt bikes. One of them was riding my stepson's bike.

"There he is," my stepson said, pointing to a floppy-haired boy, maybe eleven or twelve years old.

I approached the boy in a stern but friendly manner. I did not want to make a scene, but merely wanted to assert my adult authority to bring the issue to a quick and simple resolution.

"Is that your bike?" I asked.

The boy looked up at me with a defiant scowl. He gripped his hands tighter on the handlebars, as if to show me that he was not about to surrender this prize that he had captured.

I decided to try a more conciliatory approach.

"You know, taking something that doesn't belong to you isn't a good thing," I said.

Still, the boy said nothing. His back stiffened and his jaw tightened; he was not going to give an easy inch to this white man.

I decided to take a different tack and appeal to his sense of empathy. "How would you feel if someone bigger than you took your bike?" I asked.

Still no response.

Then, remembering Joe and the lessons of the reservation, I took a deep breath, looked the boy straight in the eye, and asked very softly, "Who's your grandmother?"

Instantly, all his defiance melted away.

Without saying a word, he got off the bike and pushed it toward me. His eyes were cast down and his manner was contrite.

The merest threat of his grandmother's involvement had struck more fear into his heart than all the words, all the moralizing, and all the implied threat of the looming presence of a large white adult standing before him.

"Hey, it's okay," I said. "Just don't do it again, and don't take things that don't belong to you."

He nodded, wide-eyed, and backed up to the safety of his friends. He stood quietly as we put the bike in the car and drove away.

❖

How unlikely such an encounter would have been in the world where I was raised. Invoking the grandmother in a confrontation would have been seen as strange, even crazy. But not in the Native world.

In the Native world, the elders are respected and honored. They are the link with the past, with the expectations of the best that has gone before. And though they may have little physical power, they have the power of true authority.

They have lived long and seen much. They are the bearers of the collective wisdom.

They understand the world in larger rhythms, because they have seen the waxing and waning of human events.

Their passions and hopes are no longer for themselves, but for the children.

Even if they have gone down the wrong road in life, their time has been full of lessons, and they want nothing more than to pass these lessons on to the children. So they speak the truth as they see it, and the children are trained to listen.

And because they are the bearers of the cultural legacy, their measure of right behavior is what you should do, not what you should not do.

Through their stories and their witness they guide the young not by threats of punishment, but by the stigma of being shamed — of being less than what you should expect of your best self.

This is what the young boy understood when I confronted him with the prospect of involving his grandmother. Because he was a good kid at heart, he did not want the shame of his grandmother's witness. The threat of my punishment meant nothing; the threat of his grandmother's disapproval meant everything.

This respect for elders does not always play out in practice, and not all elders wear the mantle of teacher in a worthy manner.

Still, the idea of the elder as the teacher and bearer of true authority is at the very core of the Native understanding of life.

And, as my friend Joe knew, the best way to keep this sacred relationship between the youth and the elders is to place them in close proximity to each other. Serving each other, brushing shoulders with each other, they overcome the natural chasm of age and foster the deeper bonds that exist between those who are weak in the eyes of the world, yet closest to the Creator.

This is not unique to the Native world. It is part of almost all traditional societies. But it is sadly lacking in our modern society.

We have marginalized the elderly, calling them "senior citizens" and warehousing them in places where taking care of their physical needs is seen as the highest expression of our concern.

Though often done with a good heart, the results, sadly, are often heartless. In caring for their physical needs, we leave them to a world of loneliness and irrelevance.

They are cared for more than they are listened to, loved more than they are respected. The children approach them more with a sense of trepidation and obligation than a feeling of expectation.

How good it would be to hear a child being told, "Go ask your grandmother," or "See what your grandfather thinks about that idea," and then to let the counsel of the grandparents stand.

That day at the feast reminded me of how rich such a life would be.

To see the soft, innocent hands of the children touching the gnarled and life-worn hands of the elders was to understand, on a deep and fundamental level, the Native belief that life is not a straight line from birth to death, but a circle where the young and old hold hands at the door of the great unknown.

As one Native woman told me years later, "We look to the children to learn what we have forgotten and to the elders to remind us of who we will become."

If we remembered only this, it would be enough.

STONES FOR THE SWEAT

All People Should Be Made to Feel Needed

Grown men can learn from very little children, for the hearts of little children are pure. Therefore, the Great Spirit may show to them many things that older people miss.

— BLACK ELK

THE SUN WAS AN ANGRY BEAD in the cloudless August sky. The bald Palouse hills were parched and brown.

I was sitting in the shell of an abandoned community sweat lodge near the small town of Lapwai, Idaho, with a man whose acquaintance I had recently made. He was Nez Perce, and this was his homeland.

He had agreed to tell me what he knew about the Nez Perce leader Hin-mah-too-yah-lat-kekt — known to us as Chief Joseph — whose story I had been commissioned to write.

Most Nez Perce I had met were rightly wary about speaking to a white man about Chief Joseph. They had seen their famous leader exploited before, and they did not want to be part of another such exploitation. But my new friend had decided to speak, and for that I was deeply grateful.

He was lineally related to Joseph, and he had grown up with stories about the revered chief. He was proud of his tradition and his blood relationship to this man who had been such a towering figure in the history of his people.

We had just returned from a walk through a lonely grassy field of river-bottom oaks and cottonwoods, where he had taken me to see a heavy iron ring nailed high on a tree trunk.

"That was placed there by Reverend Spalding back in the 1840s," he said, referring to the Presbyterian minister who had established the first missionary settlement among the Nez Perce, "so he could hang our men from it by their hands when he beat them for disobeying the white man's laws."

It was a site unknown to any history book and to many of the Nez Perce themselves. But my friend had learned about it from family stories and had shown it to me almost as an offering.

As we sat there in the protective shade of the crumbling ceremonial lodge, stories began to flow forth from him — about his grandmother and how she had been shunned by other members of the tribe for her refusal to accept the Christian ways, about what he had been told of the actual character of Joseph, about the stories he had heard recounting the way Joseph's daughter had really been killed.

The stories were loose and ruminative, as befits a conversation in the heavy hours of a sweltering summer afternoon. Soon enough they turned toward memories of his childhood.

I listened carefully, honored to be hearing his words. This man was sharing both his history and his heart. No history book could offer stories with such lifeblood coursing through them.

At one point he stood up and walked across the hard-packed dirt floor.

He pointed to a circular depression in the earth several inches deep and several feet across. "This is where the sacred fire for the sweat lodge was," he said.

"Only we young boys were allowed to gather the stones for it. We would have to look and listen and choose them. It was our duty and responsibility. No one else was allowed to do it."

He went on to tell me about how important this sweat lodge was in his life and how it had helped make him the man that he was.

We sat for the better part of the afternoon until the heat lessened and the shadows began to lengthen.

Finally, it was time to leave.

He walked to the edge of the lodge and looked out over the dun brown hills.

I remained in the shadows, watching his expressions change as he revisited his memories of this place that had been so important to him in his youth.

At last he turned back and looked at me. "I'm ready," he said, almost absently. But his heart and spirit were still somewhere far away.

We drove out through the rutted dirt tracks and headed back to the town. Neither of us spoke.

I gave him some money for groceries — a paltry gift for what he had shared with me, but it was the least I could do.

He directed me to the parking lot of an abandoned grocery store where a group of men were sitting on a crumbling concrete abutment passing around a bottle of whiskey.

"I'll get out here," he said.

"Thanks for sharing your stories with me," I said. "And thanks for showing me the old sweat lodge."

He looked at me with a wan smile. "Those were the best days of my life," he said.

Then he was gone.

-:::-

It is easy to look back at our childhood and indulge in the very human nostalgia for the simplicity of those golden days.

But, for my friend, those days had been something more. They were the days when he had first felt his responsibility as part of the human family.

For him and for those raised in his traditional way, children were not treated as "adults in waiting"; they were given responsibilities that were theirs and theirs alone.

Perhaps someone older could have done their tasks more quickly and efficiently, but speed and efficiency were not the point. The point was to give everyone a role, bound to their particular stage in life, that was theirs and theirs alone, and no one else was allowed to fulfill it.

I remember being told a story about how, in the past, the children had been charged with the task of braiding the bridles for the horses that were the key to the strength and survival of the Nez Perce people.

Perhaps they were given this task because their fingers were more agile, their eyesight more acute. But whatever the practical reasons, the essence of this responsibility was that it belonged to the children and the children alone.

They were made to feel important because they were useful and essential, and the tasks they were given were valued by the community.

And it was not only the children who were raised up in this way.

The elders, too, had responsibilities that belonged only to them and their stage in life.

They were charged with adjudicating disputes within the tribe and with carrying the history of the people in their hearts and memories, so they could pass it along by telling stories to the young.

Again, there was a wisdom and a logic to this responsibility.

Because the elders had walked far along the road of life and were no longer contending for power and influence, they were able to see with clear eyes what would benefit the individual and the community as a whole when it came to meting out justice.

And because one of the essential concerns of the aged is revisiting the past to create a coherent narrative of what their time on earth has meant, they were able to reenter the time of memory and to pass it on as if it were the present.

By raising these personal needs and skills to the status of cultural responsibility, it made the elders of any Native tribe, just as it made the children, essential and important.

It granted them an unassailable status and responsibility that belonged to them and no one else.

I often think of two small events that had profound significance in my life.

The first was a conversation I had with my teenage son and one of his friends when I asked their advice about what I should say to a gathering of a thousand fathers and sons at a wealthy boys' school in the South where I was scheduled to speak.

This was a school that had produced scientists and senators; it was where the wealthy and most influential men in the country sent their sons to receive the best education money could buy.

I could not imagine what I could say that would be of value to these fathers and sons.

So I asked my son and his friend what they would like to tell their fathers, if they were given the chance.

My son's friend, whose artistic predilections and left-of-center lifestyle had estranged him from his financial-planner father, thought for a moment and then spoke with heartfelt conviction.

"We just wish we could do something to help you," he said. "You do so much for us, but we can do nothing for you. We just wish we could do something to help you."

His father was a good parent, competent and caring. He had held his son to exacting standards of behavior, provided him with all that he needed, and been present to him all through his childhood and youth.

But the best parenting he could provide could not give his son the one thing he needed to feel worthy and significant — the capacity to be useful.

His son had been kept in the liminal status of an "adult in waiting." He had not been able to make a claim on any

identity that served a larger good and connected him fundamentally to a larger purpose and greater sense of community.

When, a week later, I passed this along to the fathers
and sons at the banquet as they sat together around their
linen-covered tables in their blazers and regimental ties,
there was an almost audible gasp when I repeated the words
of my son's friend. All across the room I could see the sons
nodding a quiet assent, while the fathers had a look of
stunned recognition.

The second event was more solitary and poignant.

My mother, widowed for several years, had finally con-
sented to move into a senior living complex.

She was a complicated woman, deeply insightful,
deeply aware, and deeply harmed by both her childhood
with an alcoholic father and the culturally constricting
times into which she had been born.

My sisters and I did what we could to make her happy
in her new life, but she saw too clearly what her world
had become. Though on the surface she made the best of
things, in her deepest heart she was inconsolable.

One day when I went to see her, I found her sitting
alone in the empty corridor outside her apartment, slumped
over in her wheelchair, crying.

I went up, put my arms around her, and asked what
was wrong.

"I can't do anything for anybody," she said between
sobs. "I'm of no use to anybody."

I tried to tell her that her life had been a gift to us all, and that her presence remained a treasure that we all valued. But I knew the truth of what she was saying. She was vestigial, in both the culture and the family.

Her children came to her to honor her; her grandchildren listened to her respectfully. But no one came to her for advice or teachings, and she had been accorded no cultural status either as the teacher of the young or as the wise, disinterested adjudicator of disputes.

How much better, how much more humane would it have been if in the winter of her life she had been given the responsibility of passing on her knowledge of the past and called upon to dispense her insights about life as more than fodder for school projects?

But she was called upon for none of this. Her cultural role was finished; the familial visits were almost more an obligation than an opportunity.

She was left alone with her memories and her small, rapidly fading life.

-:::-

Cultures, like individuals, reveal much about themselves by the way they treat the elders and the children.

In this regard, we have much to learn from Native ways. In their world it is understood that, despite the fact that the young and old are economic burdens, they have gifts to offer that only they can give.

The young offer the innocence and joy of fresh discovery.

They are a reminder of what the world was like when our hearts were pure and open, and they bring light and hope into the elders' eyes.

The elders are the mirror of who we will become.

They are the cherished bearers of our cultural memory and have a perspective on life that only the passage of time can confer. We walk in their footsteps on the journey of life.

We need to find ways in our modern society to shape these gifts into responsibilities, to make them into essential cultural roles.

In our search to provide the greatest opportunities in life for everyone, we have moved too quickly to dismantle cultural roles, because we see them as limitations on individual opportunity, not as valued responsibilities.

This empowers the strong, but it tramples upon the weak.

Cultural roles are the protectors of the weak and the guarantors of their significance and importance.

Properly framed and crafted, they enlarge the embrace of our humanity, because they allow those with no economic utility, like the young and the elders, to enrich our human experience.

This is what my friend was feeling and remembering as he stood in that afternoon sun, staring down at that small depression in the dirt on the floor of the abandoned sweat lodge and recalling his childhood.

It was a time when he had not only been loved; it was a time when he had been important.

It had been the best time of his life.

THE ELDER'S SMILE

Keep the Sacred Always on Your Lips, for What Is on the Lips Will Make Its Way to the Heart

Guard your tongue in youth, and in age you may mature
a thought that will be of service to your people.

— WABASHA

THE VAN CREAKED AND GROANED as we turned off the pavement onto the frozen dirt path. The first snows of winter had come, and ice was beginning to form on the great lake that rolled, steel gray and restless, only a few feet to our left.

The students were raucous — after all, we had escaped from the classroom. Overnight, the light and color had changed from the browns of late autumn to the muted blues and bright white of winter. The air had the fresh scent and cutting edge of snow. It had made them all giddy.

We had taken a shortcut — the "cutoff" as it was called. It was little more than a muddy, rutted dirt path that followed the route of an old trading trail that hugged the shore of the lake.

Ice-skimmed pools of standing water filled the low spots, threatening to swallow the tires of the old school van and leave us stranded in the midst of the growing northern winter.

Outside, the great lake brooded and surged. Globs of wet snow pelted the windshield. I began to doubt the wisdom of this route, even of the journey itself. But it was too late to turn back. Getting the old man to speak to the students had been a real coup for me. He was the spiritual leader of the most traditional community on the reservation — a reserved and thoughtful man — and providing the students with the opportunity to sit at his feet and listen to him tell of the old ways was what I had dreamed of since my first days on the reservation.

I gripped the wheel tightly and drove with a grim vigilance, gunning the old van through the mud and puddles and across the deadfall that the wind had blown onto the trail.

Soon even the students began to sense the difficulty of the journey. One by one, they fell silent and stared out over the icy grey waters. Only one boy, Dalton, continued to chatter.

Dalton was a good fellow — a bit of a class clown — and quite unlike the other students, whose demeanor reflected the taciturn manner of Ojibwe reality, where the great silences of the dark woods and northern distances induced a quiet in their everyday manner.

Dalton continued his running monologue, talking about how there was a spirit in the lake and how it was cool to smoke cigarettes, because tobacco was a gift of the Great Spirit.

It was all in keeping with Ojibwe belief, but coming from Dalton's mouth, all claims of spiritual insight and experience were as superficial as they were irritating. I could only assume that he was making these boasts of spiritual insight because of the man we were going to meet and his desire to impress the other students.

"Hey, tone it down, Dalton," I said.

But Dalton was having none of it. He had a captive audience, and he was going to take advantage of it.

"You know there are little people in the woods," he said. "They're like spirit beings. I've seen them. They look like lights at night. Lots of people can't see them, but I can."

His talk was making me nervous. I had been in Indian country long enough to know that you kept your counsel about spiritual forces and beings. In this land of dark forests and dark waters, some things were best left alone.

By the time we arrived at the small village where we

were to meet our host, the students had fallen completely silent except for Dalton's incessant prattling. The wind had picked up, and the snow had increased. The day had taken on an ominous edge.

Dalton kept up his running monologue as we filed off the van and into the elementary school where the old man had agreed to meet us.

We found him seated quietly in the cafeteria. He shook hands with each of the students as they came in, then gestured for us to sit in a circle facing him.

He took out his ceremonial pipe, fitted the bowl onto the stem, and filled it with the tobacco mixture he kept at his side.

He lit it slowly and deliberately and puffed it until he had created a haze of smoke. He rotated the pipe clockwise in the traditional way, holding the stem outward, stopping at each quarter turn and letting the smoke rise from the end.

When he had completed the circle, he faced it upward to the Creator, then pulled the smoke over his head with cupped hands like a man bathing himself in its presence before passing the pipe to the student next to him.

She took a few puffs, cupped the smoke over her head in a similar manner, and passed it to the boy on her left.

The pipe proceeded around the circle in this fashion. The students kept their eyes down and accepted the pipe as it came to them. They were accustomed to this ritual; it was second nature to be silent and respectful in its presence. Only Dalton violated the humility of the moment with an overly flamboyant performance of the smoking ceremony.

The spiritual leader watched quietly as the pipe passed from one student to another. A slight smile creased his lips as he watched Dalton perform his elaborate ritual.

After the pipe had made the full circle, the spiritual leader removed the bowl from the stem, placed them in their buckskin wrapping, and began to speak.

He told of the significance of the pipe ceremony and the meaning of the four directions: east, for the dawn and hope and promise; north, for the cold of winter, with its inevitability of hardship; west, for the closing of the day and the need to reflect on how we have served the people during our journey through life; and south, for the rebirth and promise that offer themselves at the end of every dark moment or event.

The students listened quietly. They knew they were being taught, and they recognized the man's authority.

"Here is how I learned," he went on. "Before you start anything — any lesson or anything — you offer this tobacco as a prayer. Tobacco is the Creator's gift. It comes from the earth and rises up to heaven. It makes you think of the Creator."

He went on to counsel them about the importance of

observing and listening. "It never stops until your last day," he said. "That's the end of your learning. Not until you have finished your last day on earth."

The students listened attentively. They had heard it before, but this man spoke with true authority. Throughout it all, Dalton was nodding his head up and down, as if offering his sage approval.

When the old man had finished, all the students except Dalton shook his hand and made their way back to the van. Dalton stayed around, carrying on about how he offered tobacco every day and how he was making his own drum and how he knew about the spirits in the lake.

The elder listened quietly, nodding and smiling as Dalton continued his discourse. When at last Dalton went back to the van, the elder came over to me.

"Who was that boy?" he asked. He had a wry smile on his face.

"That was Dalton Redfeather," I said, feeling a need to apologize for the inappropriate behavior of one of my students. "He's a good kid, but sometimes he likes to make a big deal about things he really doesn't understand. It's mostly showing off. He just needs to grow up a bit."

The elder put his hand on my shoulder. "No, that's good what he does," he said. "It's good that he says these things, even if he doesn't understand them."

"I just thought he should have been more respectful," I said.

The elder smiled again.

"He is young," he said. "He's still in practice to be a man. These things he says are like a boy trying on clothes that are too big for him. You must be patient with him. He will grow into his words. Better that he should be speaking of things of the spirit than of things of cruelty. What's on the lips makes its way to the heart."

We shook hands, and I went out to the van to begin the drive home. The wind and snow had let up, and the mood of the students was festive. They were all busy eating their bag lunches and chattering and laughing.

All except Dalton, who had fallen silent.

"Did I talk too much?" he asked me. Clearly, the elder's quiet smile and close attention to him had set him to thinking.

I thought of a dozen answers, but only one made sense.

"No, Dalton," I said. "What you said was just right."

·:⁙:·

How little we value words.

We use them unthinkingly — an unexamined extension of the endless chatter that goes on in our minds.

They are the way we connect with other people, the

way we share thoughts and observations and make ourselves known and noticed. But too often we use them without consideration, as little more than a way to fill empty space between us.

This is not the Native way.

In the Native traditions, words are like precious stones to be held up and examined, never tossed thoughtlessly. They contain power — power to console, power to hurt, power to heal.

The elder who spoke to us understood this. He chose his words carefully, always waiting until his thought had formed before offering it to the world.

For him, words were used to reveal the product of his thought, not the process.

·:::·

All those who spend long periods alone, where there is no need of words, know that after a time the chatter of the mind recedes. Thoughts become less significant, and the mind, with senses sharpened and awareness heightened, becomes a tool of pure apprehension.

When at last you have cause to speak again, the sound of your voice comes as a shock. Your words seem hard and concrete, full of containment and limitation.

They puncture the reverie that has become less like thought and more like music.

You descend, in an instant, from contemplation and observation to finite expression. Your world becomes circumscribed by your words.

The Native people understand this power of words because they understand the power of silence. Chosen carefully, words are arrows to the heart of any matter. Used mindlessly, they are a squandering of one of humanity's most precious gifts.

This is what the elder was seeing as he observed Dalton. He knew well that Dalton's words and grand gestures were empty and self-serving — a brittle attempt to draw attention to himself and portray himself in the best possible light.

But he also saw a boy with a facility with words — a gift in his community — but no respect for their power and meaning. But, like the true teacher he was, he saw Dalton's thoughtless loquaciousness as a strength to be fostered, not a deficiency to be corrected.

He knew that the power of words goes both ways. Dalton's words may have revealed a reckless indifference to considered thought, but they also shaped the direction of those thoughts. Perhaps with proper guidance Dalton could find a voice that would be of service to his people.

This is what the elder was telling me. "Be patient with

Dalton. Shape the clay of his character in the form that you find it."

He was telling me that Dalton's voicing the words of the sacred — terms we seldom use comfortably in our daily conversation — was having a profound effect on him, because it was shaping the direction of his own thought.

Wabasha, the great Dakota chief, is reported to have said, "Guard your tongue in youth, and in age you may mature a thought that will be of service to your people."

Dalton was not guarding his tongue, but the elder, in the oblique and insightful Native way, was guiding Dalton's spirit.

He knew his impact on the boy, and he knew that, by his very presence and spiritual authority in the community, he was calling forth from Dalton a languaging of the world that spoke of issues of spiritual importance.

He knew there were thoughts and ideas behind the words that Dalton was using and that, by speaking them, Dalton was bringing them alive in his heart, or at least bringing them to the portal of his heart where they knocked, seeking entrance.

What the elder was teaching me by his gentle counsel was that Dalton's words hurt no one, but, patiently tended and cultivated, they had the potential to bear fruit.

Put the sacred, kindness, and hopefulness on his lips, he was saying, and soon enough they will find a home in his heart.

II. The Native Way of Believing

We have always preferred to believe that
the spirit of God is not breathed into humans alone,
but that the whole created universe shares
in the immortal perfection of its maker.

— OHIYESA

THE OLD MAN IN THE CAFÉ

Spirit Is Present in All of Creation

From...the Great Spirit there came a great unifying
life force that flowed in and through all things — the
flowers of the plains, blowing winds, rocks, trees, birds,
animals — and was the same force that had been breathed
into the first man. Thus all things were kindred and
were brought together by the same Great Mystery.

— LUTHER STANDING BEAR

IT WAS ONE OF THOSE BREATHLESS summer noondays
when the earth is still and lifeless, and loneliness seems to
rise up from the shadows.

I was stopped at a small roadside café on the Spirit
Lake reservation in northern North Dakota. I had just
come from Fort Totten, an old military fort that stands on
the shores of Devil's Lake overlooking the broad Dakota
prairie.

Fort Totten was not an enclosed stockade of the sort one

often imagines when thinking about the forts of the American West, but rather a frontier military outpost consisting of brick barracks, dispensaries, and officers' quarters aligned in a formal geometric square around a large manicured staging area. It had obviously been intended for quartering troops and governing the surrounding territory rather than as sanctuary and protection against hostile Indian tribes.

What had drawn me to Fort Totten was the fact that it was considered one of the best preserved military forts on the northern plains — and that in 1890 it had been converted to an Indian boarding school.

I had known about the boarding schools from listening to the elders on the Red Lake reservation and had become fascinated with the dark history of this cruel social experiment.

I wanted to stand in one of these schools to see if it echoed with the haunted presence of a forgotten past. I wanted to try to imagine what it would have been like to be a child sent there unwillingly, stripped of my language, my culture, and my very relationship to the family I loved.

The visit had been sobering.

The fort was closed for maintenance, but one of the workers had kindly allowed me to wander unaccompanied around the grounds.

I had walked solemnly among the ghostly buildings, listening to my footsteps echo hollow on the worn wooden floors where frightened little children had once walked. The rows of small desks with their scratched tops seemed alive with tragic memories.

By the time I had arrived at this café, I had retreated almost completely inside myself. Images of the past had overwhelmed the present, and the haunting image of the fort set against the lonely backdrop of the great North Dakota plains had taken root deep in my heart.

As I entered the small cinderblock café and my eyes adjusted to the darkness, I saw an old man sitting by himself in a booth. He was Native, easily into his eighties or nineties. For reasons I cannot quite explain — perhaps because he seemed a part of the world that was occupying my reveries — I asked if I could sit with him.

"Sure," he said, gesturing to the seat across from him. "Sit down. I don't mind."

He was wearing a floppy fisherman's hat and drinking coffee. His movements were slow and deliberate, as befitting someone of his advanced age, but he seemed more calm and measured than infirm.

He might well have been a regular — maybe the only regular — who frequented this run-down restaurant with plywood boards over its windows and a few random tables and booths inside its darkened interior.

I slid in across from him and introduced myself. He

had lived in the area for years, he said, and had seen a lot of changes.

We shared a few pleasantries about the water level in Devil's Lake, and then I asked him whether he had gone to the boarding school at Fort Totten.

"Oh yeah," he said matter-of-factly. "I went there. I learned good English. I learned good Christian. But I am no longer myself. I am somebody else."

His comment cut me to the quick. I had seen firsthand the cultural devastation wrought in the Indian communities by the imposition of our Euro-American values and culture, and I had watched the shadows of painful memories shutter the eyes of the elders on Red Lake when the students had asked them about the boarding schools.

This man, for all his placid manner and sanguine outlook, was the very embodiment of what we as a nation had done to the Native peoples who had stood in our path as we pushed our way across the continent.

"Things have really changed," he went on. "The old ways — the way I was raised — they're gone now. They took them away from us."

He looked away and stared into the distance. I had touched something deep in him.

"My grandma," he said, "she could talk to the animals. She liked to hang clothes out on the line, stand out in the sun and the wind. She used to talk to the meadowlarks.

They would sit on the fence posts, and she would sometimes laugh and say things to them.

"I remember one day she got angry and threw a rock at one of them. I heard her scolding it as it flew away. A little neighbor girl died the next day. Grandma must not have liked what the meadowlark had to say."

He took a sip of his coffee and gazed past me almost as if I wasn't there. "I guess we forgot their language. Or maybe they just don't want to talk to us now."

"I'm sorry," I said. I could think of nothing more appropriate to say.

He hardly seemed to be listening.

"There were lots of buffalo around in those days," he went on. "My grandpa used to tell me that when something was bothering me I should go out and sit by them.

"'Don't get too close,' he'd say, 'because they can be ornery. Just be near them. Their spirits are very calm. They will understand you, and their presence will help you.'"

I looked in his ancient rheumy eyes. They were glistening with half-forgotten memories.

"They were our teachers," he said. "The buffalo would always form a circle around one of their own who was sick or wounded. They showed us how to be protectors and to care for the weak. The Creator put that knowledge into them so they could share it with us."

He lifted his coffee slowly to his lips. "I miss the old ways. The world was different then. I don't know if the world has changed, or we have."

His voice faded almost to a whisper. He was moving inside himself. I could feel it was time to leave.

"Can I pay for your coffee?" I asked.

He smiled and nodded. I left a few bills on the table and shook his hand.

His grip was soft and distant, as if he wasn't even there.

·⬧·

When I was a child my parents gave me a little black puppy.

I remember holding her on my lap in the backseat of the family car as we drove home, thinking this was the greatest gift — no, the greatest miracle — any boy could ever receive.

I named her Boots because she had white paws. It was a simple name, without cleverness or guile. But it was my name, my choice, and Boots was going to be my dog.

For the next fourteen years, Bootsie, as we came to call her, was my constant companion. She slept with me, walked with me, waited for me when I returned home from school.

She had a crooked smile and a sidewinding gait that made her seem almost comical as she ambled up to me wagging her whole back end after I returned from some adventure from which she had been excluded.

Like every child's dog, she was the greatest dog in the world.

As I neared the end of high school, Bootsie's body began to give out. Our nighttime walks became shorter and less frequent. Her step slowed; she developed a limp.

Soon she could only go a few hundred yards.

But her loyalty would not let her stay behind.

She would follow as best she could. Then, when the walking became too difficult for her, she would lift her old grey muzzle and stare at me through clouded eyes, wagging her tail gamely, as if in apology.

I would pick her up and carry her, laboring under her weight and feeling the heaving, uneven struggles of her shallow, labored breathing.

Eventually the day came, as it always does, when she looked up at me with an expression that said, "I can't do it anymore." Something passed between us, and I was called to that moment when a boy must become a man.

The next day I took her to the vet and, with tears streaming down my cheeks, held her tight as she shivered and pressed against me while the vet injected the substance into her leg that turned her from my living, breathing closest companion into an inert mass that lay lifeless in my arms.

In that instant, something deep inside me died that would never live again. In a small way, it was the same thing that had died in the old man when we imposed our language and our Western way of thinking on him and his people.

It had something to do with innocence, and something to do with faith.

·:⁝:·

I was raised to believe that we humans are the apex of creation, made, as my Sunday school classes had taught me, in the image and likeness of God — the only element of creation possessed of an eternal soul.

It was not a deeply held or well thought out conviction; it was just the way I had learned to understand the world.

But as I held my old dog in my arms and watched the light fade from her trusting, caring eyes, that conviction drained out of me as surely as the life drained out of her aged, trembling body.

I knew in that moment that I could never again embrace a belief that told me her spiritual presence and worth were inferior to mine. Her heart had been greater, her spirit purer. She had taught me about love, about faithfulness, about steadfastness and gentle caring. Her eyes had held a consciousness and understanding that was equal to mine. No one could tell me she didn't have a soul.

The residue of that betrayal — and, yes, it was a betrayal — never left me. What I heard in the old man's words and felt in his sad, wistful manner was the same betrayal, but of a far greater order of magnitude.

He had been raised in a world where the animals and

plants — indeed, the very seasons and the earth itself — all contained lessons that were there for us to acknowledge and embrace.

In their own way and in their expression of their own being, they were wiser than we were. They were teachers we needed to acknowledge.

I was reminded of a moment with a Tlingit friend of mine who had come from his home in coastal Alaska to visit me in northern Minnesota. He was in his late twenties, but was thoughtful and wise beyond his years.

He had been raised in the traditional ways by his parents and community, and he had learned his lessons well. I was honored that he had made the effort to come to visit me, and even more honored that he counted me as a friend.

It was early summer, and we had decided to go for a casual stroll down the dirt road near my home. My yellow Lab, Lucie, was happily snuffling along in front of us, nosing in the weeds and running off on occasion to chase after squirrels or chipmunks in the adjoining woods.

As we came around a corner, a huge porcupine emerged from the brush and waddled slowly across the road. Lucie had once before encountered a porcupine, and it had not gone well.

I quickly called her to me and held her back as the porcupine completed its journey across the road to the brush on the other side.

"Man, those are nasty little suckers," I said, thinking of

the hours I had spent pulling quills out of Lucie's nose and mouth with pliers.

My friend shook his head. "Porcupines aren't nasty," he said. "They have the power to hurt, yet they never bother anyone. They take care of their young, and they only use their strength when they're attacked. No, porcupines aren't nasty. They're kind."

I couldn't help but smile. Without giving it a second thought, I had been seeing the world from my own point of view; the porcupine only had meaning to me in relation to my own experience.

Yet here was a young man, not yet thirty, who saw the world not as a series of objects that gained their identity by how they impacted him, but as a series of subjects with inherent knowledge that was present to teach us if we opened ourselves to the lessons they had to offer.

For him, like the old man in the café, the world was alive with presences, and it was second nature to see the being and character in each of those presences.

-:::-

Luther Standing Bear, the great Lakota chief, put it succinctly: "Everything was possessed of personality, only differing from us in form. Knowledge was inherent in all things. The world was a library, and its books were the stones, leaves, grass, brooks, and the birds and animals that shared, alike with us, the storms and blessings of earth."

This is the world my friend saw, the world the old man remembered, the world I wish I had been given when I was growing up.

I imagined a childhood alive with this kind of understanding, where the world is a vibrant, living place filled with lessons in the land and its creatures — where buffalo teach us about protection and calm by the way they surround the weak and infirm in times of crisis; where porcupines show us the humble use of strength and personal power; and where our dogs teach us about faithfulness by their steadfast and unwavering love.

Had I been granted this way of understanding, my old dog's death would not have cast me adrift spiritually, but would have made my faith stronger and filled me with reverence and gratitude for the gifts she had given me.

She would have lived inside of me as a mentor and a teacher, not as a wound that would never be healed.

Our Western way has sent us in a bad direction where our dominance as a species is presumed without question. Whether we see ourselves as the image and likeness of God or the high point of evolution, we still see ourselves as the apex, the culmination. Everything else is lesser.

Soon enough we lose the heart to be listeners and learners. Without thinking, we reduce the world around us to a series of objects. We do not see the "thou" in our fellow creatures, only the "it."

How I wish we were raised with a constant awareness of the spirit in all living creatures — where the world is seen as our teacher rather than as a template on which we can impose our will.

How I wish we as a people had learned this from the old man and his people instead of trying to kill it in them.

Perhaps it is not yet too late for us to embrace these lessons.

It requires only that we begin to see the world and all it contains as acting upon us, rather than us acting upon it, and to cultivate the fine attention and mindfulness that comes from seeing everything as alive with its own inherent presence.

It means learning to listen before speaking, to observe before knowing, to recognize that we came last in creation and that all that was here before us had its own rules and its own knowledge.

It is the way of reverence and humility, of seeing the "thou" in all of creation.

We must learn this, or the earth may teach it to us. And, like the meadowlark that upset the old man's grandmother, what the earth has to say may be something we don't want to hear.

STOPPING THE BLOOD

We Are a Part of Nature, Not Apart from Her

> We were content to let things remain
> as the Great Spirit made them.
> They were not, and would change the rivers
> and mountains if they did not suit them.
>
> — CHIEF JOSEPH

I WAS SOMEWHERE NEAR the Missouri River, just inside the boundary of the Standing Rock Lakota reservation on the border of North and South Dakota.

The heat was insupportable. I could not drink enough water, could not keep a towel wet enough around my neck to ward off the searing pain of the relentless summer sun.

The temperature registered 112 degrees. The wind burned like the devil's breath.

I had stopped at a small old-time grocery store with a few poorly stocked wooden shelves and an old cash register with mechanical keys. It served the local reservation population, mostly by selling the kids bags of chips, candy bars, and soft drinks. Wrappers and cans and bottles lay discarded in the ditches and on the sides of roadways.

It was not the kind of rest stop I wanted, but I was desperate for some relief from the heat. And I was more than a little apprehensive about the drive ahead of me on the lonely highway that snaked into the distance through the empty, baking, treeless hills.

But what made me the most apprehensive was a feeling of almost abstract dread that something was out of balance. The land was too hot, too dry, even for this season. Something was frightfully wrong.

The locals had noticed it, too. Since I had arrived on the reservation a few days before, all the talk around the tables and in the cafés had been of drought.

Ranchers were trucking barrels of water out to their livestock to keep them from dying in the heat. Farms in the eastern flatlands were in danger of losing their irrigation.

The great Missouri River itself, the *Mni Sose*, the "Bringer of Life," was being taxed to its limits despite the best efforts of the U.S. Army Corps of Engineers to regulate its flow through an elaborate system of dams and reservoirs. The papers were full of dire prognostications and opinions.

I purchased a newspaper and a bottle of water and sat down on an old oil drum beneath an overhang in front of the store. I wanted to catch up on the latest about the drought and wait out the worst of the afternoon heat.

An old man was sitting nearby on a bench, quietly

occupying himself by constructing a cigarette from some rolling papers and a package of Top tobacco.

Like many Native men in the high plains and cattle country, he had taken on the trappings of the western cowboy, with a pearl-buttoned shirt, old Levis, and pointed-toe cowboy boots.

But it was not the irony of his outfit that caught my attention. It was the fact that he was wearing a long-sleeved shirt and had it buttoned all the way up to the collar. That anyone would wear such an outfit in this unrelenting heat seemed inconceivable.

I smiled at him, and he nodded slightly before going back to the task of constructing his cigarette.

"Any good news?" he asked when he saw me open the newspaper.

"Not much," I answered. "It looks like the farmers are in trouble. The reservoirs are drying up."

He nodded, then pulled some shards of tobacco from the end of his cigarette and wetted it with his lips.

"Damming a river is like stopping the blood in the veins," he said. "It's bound to cause trouble."

⋯⋰⋯

It would have been easy to dismiss his observation as a glib analogy or a bit of romantic anthropomorphizing.

But it was neither.

He had been raised in the Native way of understanding, where we humans are not apart from nature, but are a part of her.

For him, it was just common sense: by understanding ourselves we could understand the rest of nature, just as by understanding the rest of nature we could understand ourselves.

It brought to mind my first encounter with Taoism as a young college student.

As I sat, entranced, reading the magical words of the *Tao Te Ching*, I felt as though a shaft of light had entered my philosophical and spiritual universe.

Here was a way of understanding that was not based on some overlay of philosophical precepts or moral commandments, but was drawn from clear and simple observation of the natural world.

To hear that water had wisdom because it moved around obstacles and did not contend, or that a true leader should learn from the sea, which draws all waters to it by taking the lowest place, was not so much a revelation as a confirmation of what I had known and felt but never been able to articulate. It was nature as teacher.

Later in life, when I came upon the Native way of thinking, I was struck by how much it had in common with the Taoism that had so captivated me in my youth.

Like Taoism, it was based on understanding ourselves

as a part of nature and learning from it, not mastering it. But in the Taoist way, nature is a passive force, an indifferent teacher that embodies principles that reveal a right relationship to life.

In the Native way, nature not only offers principles that serve to instruct and illuminate right behavior; it contains actual teachings in the powers and presences of the land and all of creation that lives upon it.

It says, "Look to the tree as a lesson in praise, because it always holds its arms to the sky, even in the most powerful storm. Learn humility in the face of success from the turning of the seasons. Learn watchfulness from the wolf, faithfulness from the dog, different ways of parenting from the oriole and the eagle."

Each creature, each moment has a teaching to offer.

It is not a matter of spiritual discernment; it is a matter of mindful attention.

This is the way the old man understood the world.

For him, the river, like the tree or the mountain, was alive with an inherent knowledge. It is not alive in the way I understood, where there is a consciousness that can be discerned by the light that disappears from the eyes at the point of death.

Rather, it was alive in the sense that it possessed an interior set of characteristics and behaviors that reflected the rules by which it operated and lived out its span of time.

It was not conscious of itself; it was conscious in itself. It was alive with the presence of being.

This is what the old man was seeing when he looked at the river. The river, like the human body, had its own set of rules and behaviors that were inviolable, and to stop or alter its course was a violation of those rules.

Had he possessed the language or the scientific education, he could have talked about the strain on the ecosystem or the destruction of habitat for wildlife by the constant changing of the levels of water in the reservoir and tributaries. But that was not his way.

He was a listener and observer, not an analyst or a scientist.

When he said, "Damming a river is like stopping the blood in the veins," he was speaking as one who had learned nature's lessons.

It was an ecology born of observation, not analysis.

I could not help but think of one of the most prescient passages from the *Tao Te Ching*:

Conquering the world and changing it,
I do not think it can succeed.
The world is a sacred vessel that cannot be changed.
He who changes it will destroy it.
He who seizes it will lose it.

As an observation, it may not be scientific, any more than the observation made by the old man on the bench was scientific. But, like the old man's observation, it contains a wisdom well worth learning.

As Chief Joseph, the great leader of the Nez Perce, said, "The white man has more words to explain how things look to him. But it does not take many words to speak the truth."

The old man, in his simple quiet way, was speaking the truth. And no scientist or analyst could have said it more eloquently.

III. The Native Way of Dying

It is good to have a reminder of death before us,
for it helps us to understand
the impermanence of life on this earth,
and this understanding may aid us
in preparing for our own death.

— BLACK ELK

GRIEF'S EMBRACE

Family Is All Those We Hold in Our Heart

The ground on which we stand is sacred ground.
It is the dust and blood of our ancestors.

— PLENTY COUPS

THE WIND LASHED COLD AND HEARTLESS from the distant Canadian prairies. Shards of cold, wet snow cut the skin like bits of glass.

It was November, and I was with a group of people in a Quonset hut on the Red Lake reservation. We had come to pay our respects to a young man who had died the week before in a car accident. There were probably sixty of us; I was the only white person present. We sat in folding chairs on a cold concrete floor. The casket stood open in front of us, veiled with blue lace.

The man who was being buried had just turned thirty. He had been a student of mine — a lonely and troubled boy, seldom in class. I remembered him best for the time I had gotten him out of jail.

He had been arrested for some act of public drunkenness. He had no family or, if he did, they were no longer part of his life. Mostly he stayed with aunts and friends and other people's grandmothers or in abandoned houses and on roadsides.

He was a survivor — a hustler and a con man with a grin as big as the world. But on the day I had bailed him out, he had been a small and frightened boy, though by the time I had dropped him off in front of a house where he thought he could stay, he was full of his old bluster and swagger — a bravado and braggadocio as hollow as an echo.

I had last seen him only a few weeks ago. Years had passed, and he was now a man with a wife and two children. He still had the con-man smile, but there was a new gratefulness in his eyes. He had known the sorrows of abandonment during his childhood, and he took his parenthood seriously.

"I'm working for Red Lake Builders," he'd said. "Three years now," as if holding a job was a day-by-day accomplishment, like an alcoholic staying sober. "I just made foreman."

I clapped him on the shoulder. "Good work," I said. "You've done okay for yourself."

He smiled. I was still the teacher, and my approval made him proud.

But I was the one who had felt most proud. I had seen

a boy become a man — a lost child gather a family around himself and claim his place on the earth. Perhaps my touch had played a small part in this. And even if it hadn't, the wound I had carried in my heart for him had been healed.

But now the wound was opened again as I sat in this cold Quonset hut, so full of cigarette smoke that my eyes burned, watching as one more of my students — one of my children — was laid to rest before his time.

Despite my friendship with a few of the people, I felt out of place. There is a fine line between honoring and being witness to something that is not yours to see.

The great arcing building was hollow and empty. It had the feel of a converted repair garage for heavy equipment. The walls were chipped fiberboard, rising white above the cold concrete floor. Dim fluorescent lights flickered from the ceiling.

There were no windows, no warmth, just the high cold illumination of those spectral lights, and below it, against one of the curved walls, the casket, with the body shielded from clear view by that veil of blue lace.

Beside the casket, brown Masonite folding tables were set along the wall. A few sympathy cards were spread out across the surface, along with a sparse scattering of flowers purchased at a grocery store and placed in makeshift vases.

In the corner near the door, wooden boxes, packing crates, and a rolled-up tumbling mat were shoved against a foosball table, making a haphazard pile of objects that would be pulled out again as soon as the funeral was over.

At the far end, against the flat back wall, stood another line of Masonite tables covered with plastic food containers, cooking pots, and battered aluminum cake pans wrapped with foil.

In the center, beneath the cold fluorescent lights, the mourners sat quietly on rows of folding chairs in front of the casket, talking softly among themselves, smoking cig-arettes, and drinking Styrofoam cups of coffee and cans of Coke and Mountain Dew.

A slow, low dirgelike prayer was being chanted by the headman, who was seated in the front row. It was almost inaudible — part recitation, part song. Occasionally, low laughter rose up from somewhere among the folding chairs. Children ran across the floor, their footsteps echoing in the hollow emptiness of the Quonset space.

Except for my red jacket, it was all jeans and grey hooded sweatshirts or black nylon baseball jackets with logos of powwow groups and alcohol-rehab programs. Men wore baseball caps with insignias from logging companies and auto-repair shops. Women wore jeans or sweatpants and heavy, shapeless jackets.

A few of the teenage girls had on floor-length out-of-style velveteen dresses bought at secondhand stores or left over from some long-forgotten school dance. They walked around in heavy shoes, whispering to each other and chasing after their toddling children.

At intervals I didn't understand, the dirge stopped, the shaking of a rattle began, and we all stood. The chant took on a singsong edge, moving from high to low, before returning to its inaudible murmur as the rattle stopped and we all took our seats again.

Every few minutes the door to the Quonset opened, and the cold winter light shafted in as someone entered or left. Smoke curled to the ceiling and floated like captured fog around the humming lights.

The dirge continued, as did the standing and the sitting and the rattling. At a certain signal, the chanting stopped, and an old woman who was assisting the headman stood up. She walked with a hobble, as if one leg were shorter than the other. Her pale sweatshirt was covered with coffee stains.

She gestured us to the food tables, and we all lined up to fill our plastic plates with wild rice and macaroni casseroles, pieces of venison, fry bread, white-bread baloney sandwiches, potato chips, Rice Krispies bars, gumdrops, hard candies, and Oreo cookies.

At the end of the serving table each person stopped to scrape a bit of food from their plate into a green garbage bag propped up inside a cardboard box, so that the spirit of the deceased might have food on its journey to the afterlife.

I tore off a chunk of fry bread, tossed it in, and pushed a bit of baked beans in with my fork. An old man across from me dropped pinches of tobacco in the bag; young children poured in offerings of Mountain Dew and Pepsi, then looked up at their mothers for approval.

We milled and gathered. I saw some of my other students, now grown to men and women, with their families or alone. We talked a bit, then returned to our seats, where we each ate quietly. There was a heavy silence to the gathering, punctuated by an undercurrent of casual joking and laughter. It was the solemnity among close friends. You could not suppress the sense of community that lay at its core.

When the eating was over, the old woman stood up. "I want you to come up now," she said. "The friends and relatives first. If you got glasses, you got to take them off so he can recognize you. If you got a little kid, or if you're pregnant, you don't come up, because we don't want their little spirits to get scared. Then the family, I want you to come up last. You put some charcoal on your forehead. The rest of us will be up here to support you."

My student's mother, whom I had never met, was swaying in her chair like someone about to faint. Some people put their arms around her. A young girl went up behind her and began to braid her hair.

One by one, we filed up. A circle of ferns marked the

floor around the casket. The old woman pulled back the blue lace veil. The body was clothed in a leather jacket and a baseball cap. People stood over the corpse, touching the hands, kissing the cold lips.

When it was my turn, I placed my hands on my student's gloved hands and tried to bring a memory of his smile into my mind. I could hardly recognize him through the embalming. He had died in a car accident, and his face was a grotesque, inflated caricature — skin stretched flaccidly over balls of wadded cotton. On his cheeks were perfect circles of bright red rouge, as if painted by a clown or an old lady with a dime-store makeup kit.

I paid my respects and moved off to stand near the foosball table and the tumbling mat.

When all the guests had filed by, the family gathered around the body. It was the same as at all funerals, when those closest to the dead are faced with the closing of the casket. I looked away, trying to give them the privacy of their grief.

But many of the mourners had stayed close by. They gathered around the family in a tightening circle, literally holding them up. They lifted the wailing mother by her arms and moved her back to her chair. Quiet hugs and whispered words were shared.

The old woman gestured to some of the younger men. They picked up their chairs and moved to the front of the room. One of them carried a powwow drum. It was about three feet in diameter, made of a wooden frame with animal skins stretched taut over the top and the bottom and held to each other by zigzag patterns of hide and sinew.

"They're gonna play four songs," she said, "for the four directions."

The drum was placed in a frame made of two-by-fours, protected on the bottom by a piece of old carpet. The young men pulled their folding chairs into a circle around the drum and sat quietly waiting for their signal to begin.

The old woman faced us. "The drum is a circle, and the circle is strong," she said, "strong in all four directions. Any of you who have lost someone, you come up and stand in a circle around the drum.

"It is okay to cry. The circle is strong. It can take your grief."

Slowly, everybody in the room began to file up. We all had lost someone.

We gathered behind the drummers, expanding the circle, until it was five or six people deep.

The lead drummer started a low beat, like rhythmic distant thunder. The others joined in, first almost inaudibly, then gaining in strength.

The lead singer held his throat, as if pulling on his Adam's apple, and began a high-pitched ululation. It was a wordless ancient song, one he had learned from the elders or heard from the birds or remembered one morning when he awoke from a dream.

The other drummers picked up the melody, following it, mimicking it, accentuating it, but keeping their voices always in unison. One took the lead, then another, each lifting his voice high above the others.

But always they returned to the common voice. It was a young voice, a strong voice, for they were young men, strong men, in their twenties and early thirties, doing what their ancestors had done before them, what they themselves had been taught as young boys. The small children crowded around, hoping to learn what they, too, would someday be called upon to do.

The singing increased in power and pitch. The black animal-skin mallets hit the drumhead in hypnotic unison, each coming in from a different angle, reaching not quite to the center, rising and falling almost in a blur. Like the voices, one would rise up, go higher, hit harder, then the others would follow.

Soon they were all hitting harder. The rhythm was stronger. The drummers' faces became contorted and strained. The drum began to bounce wildly in its two-by-four frame. In the circle, women were moving, bobbing, in an echo of an ancient dance. The men put their arms on their wives' shoulders. The little children clung tightly to their mothers' legs.

The singing rose almost to a wail. The drumming took on a dark and frantic edge, full of anguish and brutality.

Soon, without warning, the grief began to pour forth from all of us, one by one — our private grief for mothers and fathers now dead, for friends lost, for children buried in tiny graves; for this young man, dead too soon, and his young children left fatherless; for five hundred years of the heartbreak of a people; for pets lost, dreams forgotten, lives poorly spent. It was not one grief; it was all grief, come together, and none could resist its common pull.

Tears flowed. Muffled sobs came from the chests of the old men. The young men stiffened and wiped the corners of their eyes. The women wept and held each other; the children cried and stared up at their mothers. None of us could escape, and none of us wished to.

Amid the Coke cans and the cigarette butts and the half-claimed rituals reduced to gumdrops and potato chips in a green garbage bag, and the casseroles made with commodity foods, and the people who had arrived in cars with broken windows and doors held shut with bungee cords, we stood as one in the stark dim illumination of this Quonset hut, pouring our grief onto that drum.

The drummers were almost frenzied. They attacked the drum as if it were alive. It bounced in its frame like an animal trying to escape. I feared it would shatter under the rain of their frantic rhythmic blows, just as I feared we would all collapse under the weight of our common grief.

But it endured. We all endured.

Then, slowly, one by one, the drum strokes softened. The lead singer kept up his haunted ululation, but the others withdrew their voices, one at a time. The drumming continued, but with ever diminishing intensity, like thunder retreating, until it was distant and gentle, almost like an infant's heartbeat. The voices stilled, and the song became as soft as a lullaby.

We all stood, shaken, in the circle. Our breathing calmed, our hearts quieted. One by one, we filed back to our chairs. We sat with eyes down, lost in our private thoughts. We were once again separate beings.

The service went on, filled with rituals to which I had no entry.

The casket was wheeled in circles; the headman offered Ojibwe prayers. The old woman said, "The spirit is still with us until we let him out that door. Then he will be gone."

The headman chanted. The people stood in silent vigil while a ceremonial pipe was smoked so the spirit could be set free. Then the casket was carried out and placed in the pickup truck that would carry it to the grave the men had dug that morning.

I followed slowly behind as we made our way to the burial ground. Up ahead I could see the pallbearers huddled in the back of the pickup, accompanying the casket. The sleet was blinding; the wind off the great lake was cutting and vicious.

At the gravesite the headman took charge. He began his prayers in earnest. People gathered around the grave in a circle, while the young men shouted instructions to each other and lowered the casket into the hole with ropes.

The headman pointed to one of the children. "Now you kids put the flowers in."

The children filed up one by one. Some stared into the grave as they dropped their flowers. Others threw them from a distance, as if they were afraid to get too close.

"That's good, you little ones," he said when they were finished.

Then he nodded to the rest of us. "You fill it in now," he said. "You all put some dirt in. Even a handful."

There were four shovels. My student's friends grabbed them and began shoveling with the same frenzy with which they had beat the drum. It was as if they had to get the casket covered before their grief escaped.

Some jumped in the hole and began tamping the dirt around the edges. Others got down on their hands and knees and pushed the wet, muddy clay in with their hands. One by one we all took our turn, throwing cold, wet earth into the rapidly filling hole.

Someone gave me a shovel. I tossed in dirt until another

man took the shovel from me. Then I got down on my knees and began pushing the mud in with my hands.

The wet earth seeped through the knees of my pants, up the cuffs of my jacket. It soaked my gloves and froze my fingers. We worked together, the old men, the young men, the mothers and daughters, the tiny children, and the grandmothers. Some threw just a handful; others shoveled with a fury. We got the casket covered, then stood with the moist, rich earth covering our hands and clothes and knees and faces.

We had buried him. We had placed him in the earth.

The headman directed a few young men to cover the grave with a sheet. The ends were held down with dirt; then the whole surface was covered with plastic flowers.

The sleet had turned to snow. People pulled their jackets tight around them. The headman smoked the pipe, sending the smoke in the four directions, down to Mother Earth, up to Father Sky.

"Well, that's it," he said. "*Miigwech*. Thanks for coming."

I walked back to my car, with the cold earth caking on my hands. There had been no meaningful ending, but somehow it all seemed right.

It was thirty dark miles back to my home. The roads were icy, and the forests deep.

I looked at my hands and the clay that covered them,

the clay of my student's grave, the clay of his people's ancestors, the clay that would one day take their bodies and the bodies of their children and their children's children.

The old woman's words kept running through my mind. "The circle is strong. It can take your grief."

I crossed the reservation line, back into familiar country. Back into America. And as I did, something passed from me, something I could not understand. But it slipped away as surely as the spirit of my student slipped away when they wheeled his casket through that Quonset door. It was an understanding, deeper than memory, as deep as the grave we had filled, as deep as the land on which we had been standing.

I could not give it a name, but it had something to do with family, the earth, and love.

--:::--

Not long after the funeral of my student, I found myself standing in a military cemetery on the edge of a freeway in Minneapolis. My family and I had come to bury my father. He was a veteran, and he had lived a long and worthy life. His time had simply come, but for that our grief was no less.

The cemetery, like most military cemeteries, was a beautiful green expanse of ground with white round-topped gravestones marching in formation over the terrain, like the ghosts of the veterans who were buried there. It echoed of sacrifice and patriotism and peace.

The area where my father was to be interred was in a section that had recently been established to meet the burial needs of the many World War II veterans who were passing. It was flat and raw and had no trees, and was directly beneath the flight path of the jets taking off from the adjacent international airport. In clearing and preparing the ground, the bulldozers had uncovered old refrigerators and car parts. It had once been the site of a dump.

We were given a time to assemble on a road in the middle of the cemetery about a mile from the interment site. A silver hearse containing my father's body was parked at the place that had been designated for our gathering. A short distance away we could see another hearse and line of cars. Burials took place on a schedule.

We stood beside our cars as the cortege in front of us moved out and snaked its way to the interment area. While we waited, another group was lining up a block behind us, falling in, as we did, behind the hearse carrying their loved one.

A walkie-talkie squawked out a signal to the cemetery employee assigned to set our procession in motion. We drove slowly through the old part of the cemetery toward the naked plot of land designated for the new burials. Jets roared overhead, shaking the car and making conversation impossible. The traffic on the nearby freeway droned endlessly.

At the spot assigned for the ceremony — still far distant from the actual burial site — those assigned as pallbearers slid my father's casket from the hearse onto a wheeled cart that was pushed under a small canopied structure.

A short ceremony took place, interrupted several times by the roar of the jets.

My mother was given a flag, folded into a triangle in the military fashion, and a line of elderly veterans in ill-fitting uniforms who volunteered their time to serve as honor guards raised their rifles and let off three volleys of seven ear-splitting shots. They had not known my father. My father had not known them.

A recording of taps was played, and the ceremony was over.

When the service was finished, I approached the cemetery representative and said I wished to accompany the casket to the burial site.

"I'm his only son," I told him. "I want to help place my father in the ground."

He seemed surprised. The actual burial would not take place immediately, he said — apparently it was to be put off until a number of caskets were assembled — and the exact location of my father's plot would be determined based on the sequence of deaths.

We would, he assured me, be given instructions as to where to find my father's grave once the interment actually took place.

The casket carrying my father's body was taken away, and I went back to comfort my mother and be with my family.

The casket carrying my father's remains was taken away, and we were left alone with our overwhelming sense of incompletion and our unresolved sense of grief and loss.

·:·

The spring after my student's death, I went to his gravesite to pay my respects. He had been a part of my life, and I had been a part of his. His death had brought us together again, and I wanted to honor that bond.

I drove into the reservation cemetery on the rutted unpaved road. The graves were all decorated with pinwheels and dolls and bouquets of plastic flowers. It was a multicolored carnival of death celebrating the lives of those who were buried there.

My student's grave had not yet completely settled. The mound, though less than the pyramid of earth we had created with our common hands, still rose above the level ground. Winter had taken its toll on the flowers and teddy bears and photographs that had been placed there by family and friends. But like his memory, they still told their stories, though now in more muted tones.

A baseball cap — perhaps the one that had been in his casket — was on the top of the mound. Someone must have set it there recently. It would not have survived the winter winds and snows.

I walked slowly around the grave, looking at the trinkets and photos and ribbons and dolls. It was the archaeology of a life, and in its mute testimony it told me more about my student than I had ever known while he was alive.

"You were a good man, Pat," I said. "A hard case, but a good man."

My voice surprised me. It had the same tone I had used when we had last spoken those many months ago.

The wind blew soft. The scent of the lake was strong.

I adjusted the hat to make sure it was secure on the grave.

"I'm glad I bailed you out that day," I said. "You were worth it."

·:·

Several months after my father's death, using the map I had been given, I went to his gravesite and placed one of his tobacco pipes in front of his white humpbacked gravestone. He had smoked a pipe for as long as I could remember, and it had been one of his few joys as the years and his infirmity had closed in around him.

The smell of his favorite tobacco remained in the wood of the pipe. Memories flooded in as I placed it against the gravestone — my childhood rides in the back of our station wagon, his love of puns that made everyone cringe, our Friday evenings watching boxing together on our little black-and-white television.

As I was leaving, a man in a cart came up and asked me what I was doing. He handed me a sheet of regulations. One line read, "Permanent plantings, statues, vigil lights, breakable objects, pinwheels, balloons, toys, stuffed animals, and similar commemorative items are not permitted on the graves at any time."

I picked up the pipe and went home.

-:::-

Chief Joseph, a man I revere almost as much as I revered my father, said, "A man who would not love his father's grave is worse than a wild animal."

I do not love my father's grave. I do not even know my father's grave. I know only one anonymous white tombstone among thousands, where the echo of my father's memory competes with the memory of excavated refrigerator parts and the roar of jets passing overhead.

It is neither the place of his birth nor the place of his death, nor a place he held dear.

I cannot reach down and lift a piece of earth and say, "This was his land."

I do not even know that his designated plot is the actual place of his burial.

My father, in his passing, was reduced to an abstraction, a job that he performed, a service he dutifully rendered to his country with less passion than sense of obligation.

I, his only son, was not even permitted to see him placed in this indifferent earth, much less to fill the grave of his burial with my own hands.

I was left with only a mimeographed map designating quadrants, sectors, and locations of graves and the promise of the military that the land, now cleared of refrigerator parts and engine blocks, contains his remains.

-:::-

We do ourselves no service when we hide ourselves from the presence of death, and we do the dead no honor when we take from them the fullness of their lives.

I will forever have the memory of the moist earth of my student's grave upon my hands.

I have only the fading memory of my father's casket receding from sight in the back of a silver hearse.

My student's grave, covered with teddy bears and figurines and notes from his friends, is a history of his life, made manifest for all to see.

My father's grave is a cipher, democratized and stripped of individuality to emphasize the selfless nature of the service his country called him to perform.

Each is honorable in its own way. But I want more than honor for my father; I want love.

He deserves to be more than one more tombstone marching mutely over this silent ground. He deserves to be the pipe, the army hat, the ribbons, the crucifix of his earnest faith. He deserves to be the certificates of his training in first aid and his commendations from the Red Cross for meritorious service.

He deserves to be the pictures of his favorite dogs, of his children, of his wife; an old album cover of the Strauss waltzes he loved so dearly; the letter he received from Hubert Humphrey.

He deserves all this and more, and it deserves to fade with his memory and be replenished by those who honor that memory until there are no more who choose to remember or care.

And when there are no more to remember, he deserves to lie silent in earth that he loved, not in indifferent ground that he shares with car parts and old refrigerators.

·⁖·

I stand now, miles and years from the deaths of these two good men, one whose life I played a small part in shaping and one whose hand shaped the very man I am today.

In each of their deaths I felt a profound sense of loss and the deeply human experience of grief.

But my grief for my father was a lonely grief. As I stood, watching that departing hearse, I was cast back into the isolation of my own private sorrow.

My student's burial made us all one. Standing in that circle, swaying together, we were embraced in our common experience of grief. And as we threw our handfuls of dirt into his grave, in some distant fashion we buried that grief.

There is a certain nobility in the private contemplation of mortality, but there is a rich humanity in the common sharing of a deep human emotion.

My father's passing taught me something essential about death and loss.

My student's passing taught me something about humanity and life. Because of him, and the way his people shared that passing, I know what it means to be held in each other's arms.

THE LEGACY
OF THE FATHER

Our Past Is a Responsibility, Not a Burden

Death will come, always out of season.
It is the command of the Great Spirit,
and all nations and people must obey.

— BIG ELK

THERE WAS SOMETHING IN HIS EYES that kept you at a distance — something deep, troubled, intelligent, and dark. This was a young man who did not want to be reached or touched.

His father had been a widely respected member of the Native community and had died suddenly — too young — and had left his son, a grown man himself, with unresolved angers and guilt that now cast an indelible shadow over his life. He would spend the remainder of his days dealing with the ghost of a man he had loved deeply, but with whom he had not made a meaningful peace.

We were sitting in a living room, maybe ten of us — Native and white — having just finished a convivial dinner.

The subject naturally moved around to the young man's father, because he was the common thread that united us all.

Throughout the meal the son had remained silent. Wishing to engage him in the conversation and hoping to draw him out, we began telling him of our fondness and respect for his father. We were wary of lavishing too much praise on our departed friend, because we knew that part of the young man's challenge was to find a way out from under his father's shadow while still honoring the man who had raised him and shaped him.

We fumbled around, each sharing memories of the man whose absence sat at the center of the room, until a Dakota man who knew what it was to lose a father spoke up.

"You know," he said to the still grieving son, "you're lucky."

The young man, who until this time had remained politely distant, suddenly became attentive.

"Lucky?" he said. "I don't feel very lucky."

The Dakota man looked down, as if gathering himself, and spoke with an almost ritual solemnity. It was as if he were passing on knowledge from some far distant memory.

"We all must grieve," he said. "It's what makes us human, because it speaks of love. It is necessary and right to grieve for a father, a mother, an aunt, an uncle. Because we love them differently, we grieve for them differently. I feel sorry for children who have not known their father, because they cannot grieve for his death or for the death of their grandparents. They miss part of being human. You are lucky to know this grief in your heart."

-:::-

Grief is a fundamental human emotion. It is the heart's response to the experience of loss. The greatest grief is for those losses that hurt us most, and the loss of a parent, next to the loss of a child or a spouse, may be the most hurtful loss of all.

I remember the deaths of both my mother and father. Each, in its own way, affected me deeply and fundamentally. There was so much left unsaid, so many moments of regret, so many moments of joy.

As a son to my father, I carried many painful self-recriminations about how I had not shown him proper respect in my words and behavior, and how I had failed to understand the struggles he had faced as he had tried to shepherd me into a worthy manhood.

It was only as I took on the mantle of fatherhood myself that I began to realize what he had done and what he had overcome, because it was only then that I understood the challenges that fatherhood presents.

My mother's death was different, though no less intense. When my father died, it was as if the roof had been ripped off my life. When my mother died, it was like the earth had been pulled out from under me.

My young Native friend still had the foundation of his mother's presence to offer him emotional support and refuge, but he was now facing a world without the presence of the father looming over him, protecting him, challenging him, limiting him, judging him, and serving as the constant measure of his own manhood. The complex reality of the father's presence had now become an absence frozen in time, and it would remain there, like a hole in the sky, for as long as he lived.

This is what the Dakota man who offered that unexpected counsel understood. He knew that though the scream of grief is universal, the issues the young man had to confront inside that grief were unique both to the death of a father and to the man himself.

The rest of us were offering well-meaning consolation. He was shining a light into the emotional tangle that the young man had to navigate and offering him a glimpse of a way to understand and grow and heal.

·:::·

In the Native way, family relationships and responsibilities have profound and nuanced complexity.

I recall a conversation with a Nez Perce man about how

his people had traditionally defined the ideal leader. The ideal leader, he said, was an oldest son who had an older sister. Being the first son gave the boy authority and a sense of responsibility, but having an older sister kept him from becoming too full of himself, because she was always present to put him in his place when he developed an overinflated sense of his own importance.

Another Native man once told me about the responsibility he felt toward his young nephew. As the uncle, he said, it was his responsibility to be the teacher and guide to the young man. The father, he explained, was considered too close to the boy and would likely be too soft or too hard on him.

In his people's way, he told me, the father was expected to serve as a model of impeccable behavior. It was the uncle who was the counselor and confidant and the one to mentor the child during the passage from boyhood to manhood.

And the same complex relationships and responsibilities existed for the girls and women.

I once had a student who came to school without her homework. When I questioned her, she told me, "I couldn't get to it. I didn't go home last night."

"And where did you go?" I asked, taken aback by what seemed to be brazen honesty.

"I went to my auntie's," she said. "I stay there a lot."

I thought at first that this was some personal situation; perhaps she and her mother didn't get along or there were difficulties with her home life. But a few months on the reservation showed me that this was not personal; it was cultural. The auntie was another mother with full maternal authority, and it was in no way unusual for my young student or any of the students to go to their aunties for teaching, consolation, or simply a place to stay.

⋰⋱

The full complexity of the roles of times past in Native communities may not exist today, but the outlines still remain. And within those outlines are understandings that plumb a deep dimension of human experience.

The Dakota man at the dinner gathering was pointing to the unique role of the father and asking the grieving young man to honor his father's memory by embracing the unique nature of his grief.

It was a compassionate nudge toward an understanding of fatherhood, both as the gift and the burden his father had bequeathed him and the responsibility he would assume when he became a father himself.

It was a reminder that his father's death was not only a loss, it was a legacy, and that each of us, no matter how insignificant, has a crucial role to play in the great interconnected tapestry of the human family.

DONNA'S GIFT

Giving Is the Greatest Human Act

We must learn early the beauty of generosity....
Public giving is a part of every important ceremony.
It properly belongs to the celebrations of birth, marriage,
and death, and is observed whenever it is desired
to do special honor to any person or event.

— OHIYESA

It was, I believe, a Saturday morning when the call came.

Though the telephone — the "reservation tom-tom" — was the primary means of communication in Indian country, my Native friends knew I was no lover of phone conversations, so I seldom received calls from even the closest of them.

So it came as a surprise when I picked up the phone and heard an Indian voice. It was a woman I barely knew who lived in a distant city. She was brief and to the point and spoke with the brittle formality of one masking heavy grief. She said her mother, Donna, had died and asked if

I would attend the burial. The funeral service was to be a family event, but her mother, she said, would have wanted me at the gravesite.

"Of course I'll be there," I said. Donna had been one of my closest and most valued friends in Indian country. It was an honor to be asked.

I had gotten to know Donna almost by accident. She had been assigned to serve as the female chaperone on trips I took with my students. She was very much a follower of traditional Ojibwe ways, having been raised in an Ojibwe-speaking home with traditional Ojibwe values.

She had a gentle heart, a comforting, motherly manner, and a ready laugh that was alive with delight and surprise. The students loved her.

In her person and her manner, she was a constant reminder of what it meant to be Ojibwe and who they were expected to be.

I loved traveling with Donna. She made up for my errors of being too strict or too lenient, because she did not have rules; she had true authority. A glance, a withholding of approval or affection, or even a turn of the head was all she needed to set a student straight, and it was always followed by a giggle and a knowing, caring smile. Though she and I were about the same age, I looked upon her almost as a mother.

After I finished my time on the reservation, I saw Donna only on rare occasions. But we shared the easy bond of people who had been longtime traveling companions and had known the joys and difficulties of caring for a group of young people. So when I would run into her on the reservation or in town, it was like a reunion. We joked, we joshed, and she would slap at my shoulder with mock outrage when I teased her about something.

And always there was laughter.

The last time I had seen her she was sitting in a car outside a small gas station waiting for a friend. She was staying in the car, she told me, because she was barely able to walk. Always a heavy woman and afflicted with various ailments and injuries since childhood, she now got around in a wheelchair, if she went out at all.

It was a sad revelation. Though we had often joked about how we were getting old whenever we saw each other, her deterioration had been alarmingly rapid. It was clear that this was not just some temporary setback. She would never walk again.

I had leaned in and given her a hug — a rare act I seldom performed with Ojibwe women, whose willing laughter and joking manner often masked a deep personal reticence and physical propriety — and we had parted as we always did, with a feeling of warmth for each other and pleasure that the bond between us remained strong.

I did not expect that it was the last time I would see her alive.

The burial took place on a windswept promontory that overlooked the endless expanse of pines and tamarack that stretched into the brooding distances of the great Minnesota north. Large dark birds circled over the forest treetops. The wind blew lonely from the far distant Canadian prairies.

The gathering was small. Scattered groups of people stood at a distance from the gravesite, talking softly and smoking cigarettes. The long, low doghouse-like spirit houses of the dead stood in rough formation along the sandy loam and wire-grass hilltop. This was a burial ground, not a cemetery; a community of the dead.

I stayed in the rear, feeling like an outsider — even an intruder — who had been granted an unearned right to be present at something that was deeply private and not meant for white eyes. This was beyond familial; this was ancient. I was in the presence of the ancestors. I was standing on hallowed ground.

The burial took place in the traditional manner. The young men placed the casket into the grave they had dug that morning, and each of us shoveled a bit of dirt onto the casket before the young and strong finished the task of filling the hole with earth.

As the ceremony drew to a close, Donna's daughter approached and handed me a white plastic bag. "This is for you," she said. "My mom said she wanted you to have it."

I did not think it appropriate to open the bag at the gravesite. So I thanked her, shoved it in my jacket, and walked back to my car to begin the sixty-mile drive back through the forests to my home.

Once alone in the car I opened the bag to see what it was that Donna had wanted me to have. Inside were a pair of hospital socks, a pack of handkerchiefs, a small jack-knife, a package of combs, a pair of leather work gloves, and some unopened pillowcases.

For a brief moment I was confused. What were these things, and why had Donna wanted me to have them? I searched in vain for some common theme that united them or some symbolic significance that addressed our time together. But I could find none.

Then a rush of understanding came over me. These were the objects Donna could find in her hospital room. She had folded them and arranged them lovingly in the only package she could find, and she had given them to her daughter to give to me.

Tears welled up in my eyes. This dear woman, whom I saw so seldom, while lying near death in her hospital bed, had shaped a gift for me from the only items she had within her reach.

I set the bag on the seat beside me. Memories of Donna's gentle smile and mirthful laughter rose up in my memory.

This was the Indian way made real. When significant events take place, you do not receive gifts; you give gifts. It is a way of honoring and showing appreciation for those who have shared your life's journey. It is an act of humble acknowledgment and gratitude, a bearing witness to their significance in your life.

Donna's gift was her way of thanking me for my friendship.

Over the years I have developed a great respect for this Native tradition of giving. From Chief Joseph's Nez Perce funeral, where all his earthly possessions were given away to mourners; to a struggling Lakota family on the Pine Ridge reservation spending all its money to provide a feast for the entire community when a family member died; to Donna's simple gift of what she had within reach in her hospital room, giving and sharing is at the very heart of the Native way of life.

I have heard anthropologists speak of this tradition as a demonstration of wealth and power and status. And in some instances, that might be true.

But where was Donna's wealth? Where was Donna's power?

She had no power to demonstrate. She had no status to protect. She gave simply to express her appreciation and respect and love.

Donna's death saddened me in many ways. And it was

not just sadness for her death, though that sadness, like the sadness at the passing of any friend, was deep and real. It was sadness that her quiet, unseen grace and dignity would forever remain unknown to all but those close to her.

She represented the best of Native people and Native ways and, like all of the good, caring Native people across this land, was completely invisible to the America that I call home, where Indians are mythologized and pathologized into something that completely distorts the beauty of who they really are.

Donna was not an idea, a philosophy, a member of a bygone race, a welfare queen, a drunk, a wise woman, or a recipient of large checks from casino earnings.

She was a friendly woman with a willing laugh, a mother's concern for all the kids in the neighborhood, and a daughter's love and respect for her aged parents.

She was overweight, played bingo, drank bad coffee, loved fry bread, and gave away her money, food, and anything else she had to friends and people in need.

She believed in the presence of spirit in her dogs and cats and the animals her family hunted and felt that the spirits of her ancestors both guided and challenged her.

She was happy having little, was humble in the presence of others, and did not speak unless she had something to say. Though she loved a good joke, she was never caustic or cynical. I never heard her raise her voice in anger.

And while she lay dying, she gathered together little gifts to be handed out to her friends at the time of her passing.

She was as real as a person can be, and the very embodiment of the Indian spirit of giving, where a gift is more than an act of generosity; it is a way of saying, "Thank you."

She was my co-worker, my mentor, my traveling partner, and my friend.

I will always miss her.

IV. THE NATIVE WAY OF KNOWING

We should understand well that all things
are the work of the Great Spirit.
We should know that he is within all things:
the trees, the rivers, the mountains, and
all the four-legged animals and all the winged peoples.

— BLACK ELK

THE HIP BONE

We Are Children of the Earth; We Walk in the Footsteps of Those Who Came Before

The white man does not understand America.
He is too far removed from its formative processes....
Men must be born and reborn to belong. Their bodies
must be formed of the dust of their forefathers' bones.

— LUTHER STANDING BEAR

I AM STANDING IN A LONELY FIELD, far from the nearest road, in the open prairie country of northwestern Minnesota. Just beyond me, the Ojibwe man who brought me here is overseeing the reburial of the bone fragments of two young girls, maybe fourteen or fifteen years of age, that were unearthed by a farmer during an excavation on his land.

We know they are girls and their approximate ages because modern science, with its tools and technologies, has analyzed their anatomical structure and drawn this conclusion. Yet beyond those facts we know nothing about them. They are thought to have lived over a thousand years ago, members of a culture now faded into the mists of history.

My journey here began this morning when I had coffee with the man who is performing the reburial. He had sought me out because he knew of my work among Native people. He said he liked what I had done and wanted to meet me. I was honored by his request and more than happy to comply.

He had arrived at the coffee shop with his son — a young, thin, quiet man full of attentive respect for his elders and his Native tradition. He was assisting his father in his work as the state compliance officer for the reburial of remains of Native people dug up during excavations of highway roadbeds, the digging of foundations for shopping malls, and the plowing of fields all across Minnesota.

He was learning the proper ways of reinterment in the only manner that such ways can be learned — as an apprentice to those who had already been taught by their grandfathers and grandmothers before them.

As we sat at the table together — men of different races, different ages, different pasts, and different lives — we felt the common kinship of fathers and sons trying to do what is right in a complex world.

"It's hard," the man said. "These aren't just 'remains' to me. These are people."

In the state's eyes, he was helping to fulfill a legal obligation mandated by federal law. But for him, this was far more. He was doing his best to give proper respect to husbands, wives, children, and elders whose bodies had been disturbed in their resting places by the onward push of modern civilization.

But in his heart the task ran deeper still.

He was providing peace to spirits — a notion not part of any job description or even any sense of moral propriety and obligation, but part of the reality for anyone, especially a Native person, who is alive to the mystery that lives beneath the practicalities of everyday life.

This man experienced that mystery on a daily basis, and now he was showing his son the proper way within his tradition to honor and give rest to those spirits.

He told me of his concerns — of how he sometimes doubted his worthiness; of how the loneliness of the task sometimes became a burden almost too great to bear; of how he worried that the spirits would take offense if he did not do things in the proper way or with a proper heart.

That very afternoon, he said, he was going out to reinter the remains of two young women from a culture at least a thousand years old. It was in a rural area on the edge of the prairies a hundred miles west of us, almost to the North Dakota border.

"Would it be all right if I went along?" I asked.

It was a forward request, but a Native man who brings his son to meet you is showing a respect that speaks of trust in the quality of your heart and character. I did not think he would take offense.

"That would be good," he said simply.

And so we found ourselves in this field, miles into the empty farmland of northwestern Minnesota, amid bur oak, sumac, and tall grasses.

The farmer who had unearthed the bones was here also — lanky, strong, with hands like tree roots — along with a tall, quiet Dakota man who had been called to perform the actual ceremony of interment and several young Ojibwe men and women in their late teens and early twenties who had come to witness and assist in the reburial.

The women were quiet, as is often the Ojibwe fashion. The young men had short-cropped hair and wore baseball caps cocked sideways, baggy shorts, baggy shirts, and black tennis shoes with no laces.

To a person on the street they would have seemed like gangsters, displaying by their appearance a dark defiance and thinly veiled sense of menace. But here, in this field far from their homes, they seemed small and humble and respectful in the presence of death.

We stood in the warm summer drizzle, fighting off the mosquitoes, as the reburial took place.

The man who had invited me gave a short talk about the site, about how it had been found, about what little we knew of the people who had lived here over a thousand years ago, about how it would now be recorded and protected in accordance with state law. He had his son give us each a pinch of tobacco to throw in the grave, then turned the ceremony over to the Dakota man.

The Dakota man instructed my friend's son in the proper way to offer the pipe to each of us. Those of us who chose to smoke did so in turn, offering the smoke upward to the sky as a gift to the Great Mystery and an honoring of the spirits of those people whose bones were once again being laid to rest.

The Dakota man spoke — his voice was soft and his manner was kind — reminding us that the four directions were like the seasons of life and that culture was not something in the past, but something alive today.

The young Ojibwe men took off their caps. The farmer stood with his head bowed. The young girls cast their eyes downward and listened attentively. Then we each walked up and circled the grave, sprinkling our tobacco in it as we passed.

When we had finished, the farmer climbed on his yellow front-end loader and fired it into life. The pounding surge of the diesel engine cut through the silence of the field and the soft whisper of the rain. He shoveled the dirt — the same dirt that he had excavated, now sifted clean of human remains — into the hole.

The young men took shovels and did what they could

to reshape the mound into its original form. The young girls held their shirt collars tight against the rain. The Dakota man remained at a distance, watching quietly.

Soon the rain increased, and thunderstorms spit from beyond the horizon. It was time to go.

Another short prayer, and we all hurried back to our cars at the edge of the field, lost in our own thoughts and struggling to sort out the feelings that were coursing through us.

Who, besides us, knew what had taken place here?

Who, besides us, cared?

The state would be satisfied to see the site marked on an archaeological map. The farmer was satisfied to know he had done the right thing and could get on with his life.

But beyond that, there were only we few witnesses, the empty sky, and the distant birds circling over some distant prey.

-:::-

How wrong it felt to watch the bones of children being placed in a pit and covered by a front-end loader. These bones had once been young girls who had run and laughed and played on this very land.

They had chased after boys, worried their parents, sat with their grandmothers, and had dreams of bearing children. They had stared out over these same fields, watched the same sun set in the west, and covered their heads against the same warm summer rain.

Who were they? How did they live? And are their spirits still present, as my friend who oversaw the burial believes?

I do not know. I cannot know. I can only bear witness and hope that my witness somehow does honor to their memory.

·:·

We are quick to draw lines where our awareness stops. Our streets, our alleyways, our history on the land — these form boundaries enough for us.

But there are truths that lie beneath our consciousness, just as there are truths that lie beneath our feet. That we do not know them does not mean that they do not exist, only that we do not have the patience and humility to hear.

Many years ago I stood in a dry creek bed in Alaska north of the Arctic Circle, staring out over a river of stones that wound, sinuous, into the purple arctic twilight.

Perhaps it was the strangeness of the setting, perhaps it was the power of the moment, but, as I stood there, those stones began to speak. It was a clacking sound, a clattering sound, like the fluttering of wings, the descent of birds, the pounding of a hundred thousand hooves across the frozen tundra.

I could not name it, but neither could I deny it. It came to me through senses unfamiliar, claiming me with a knowledge I did not know. That it was not within my rational understanding did not make it any less real.

The bones of these girls and the forgotten thousands of people who walked on these lands before us and gave their bodies and spirits to this soil speak with that same voice. We hear it, if we hear it at all, with a sense that lies far below our conscious awareness.

·:·

The wheel of civilization turns. Cultures rise and fall, lifting some lives up and leaving others buried and forgotten.

Two hundred years ago, the ancestors of the men who performed the reburial ceremony had been sworn enemies, fighting each other and taking each other's lives.

One hundred fifty years ago, my ancestors and the ancestors of the farmer who now claims this land had supplanted them both, tilling the fields, feeding their families, fulfilling the biblical injunction to make the land bear fruit.

There are no villains here among the conquerors and the conquered — only men and women doing their best to care for their loved ones and to raise their children into hopeful and promising lives. That their ways differed, and that one prevailed while the other faded, is but the sad and inevitable outcome of the winnowing forces of civilization.

The girls we buried are anonymous. They will remain anonymous. They have no families to remember them, no parents to grieve for them. We cannot, and will not, know their names. The human beings they once were and the lives they once lived will be forever forgotten, despite our best efforts to honor their memories.

But the dead are not so easily buried. Their laughter, as well as their bones, inhabits this soil.

It is the Native way to acknowledge this truth.

It is a deeper truth than we understand — deeper than a simple attachment to place, deeper even than the belief that the land where they were born was given them by the Creator.

It is a belief — even an understanding — that in our death we return to the soil; that who we are, in body and in spirit, nourishes the plants that grow up to feed the animals that give their lives to feed our bodies, so that our children and the children of all the creatures that share this earth live inside of us, even as they live inside the trees and plants and animals around us.

We are common kin, born of a common earth, far deeper and far richer than the movements of people and events that take place upon the surface of creation.

That is why we feel the presence of ghosts when we stand on hallowed ground — the battlefield at Gettysburg, the hard stones of Dachau, the rocky promontory of Masada, the lonely hilltop at Wounded Knee.

In those places the presence of the dead is so strong that it cannot be ignored.

Yet these ghosts are everywhere, and that we do not hear them except as faint and distant echoes does not mean that they do not exist.

Perhaps it would be too much if we could truly hear the deep voices of the world around us, and we would cover our ears in terror, like the deaf man who, hearing for the first time, covers his ears to block out the unbearable cacophony of life. Perhaps if every gully cried out to us with the laughing and clacking of stones, we would go insane.

The hip bones of those girls sang in a tiny voice — sweet, pure, beyond our hearing. We do them no justice if we deny that song or think that it sings only a lament for a lost and defeated culture. Those girls are our ancestors, part of the earth that nourished us and gave us life.

It is good that we were here to bear witness to their lives. We need to keep them alive in our hearts, even if we cannot hear the laughter in their voices or the soft and distant music of their song.

VOICES IN THE STONES

Everything We Turn Toward the Creator Is a Prayer

We recognize the spiritual in all creation
and believe that we draw spiritual power from it.

— OHIYESA

THE PRAIRIE AROUND ME stretches wide and peaceful as far as the eye can see. It rolls gently under the blue vault of the warm September sky here in this quiet land of fields and farms in the southwest corner of Minnesota, just east of the South Dakota border. I am here with Raymond and Martin, two Tlingit friends of mine who are visiting from the small coastal village of Yakutat in southeastern Alaska.

Raymond is a quiet man in his late sixties who carries the burdens of a long life spent fighting for the rights of his people against cruise lines, oil tankers, and insults against the environment.

He also carries the scars of difficult times in Vietnam and the weight of childhood experiences in the Native boarding schools.

He is a survivor with a deep gentleness in his heart.

Martin, his son, is a young man just coming into his own, who carries burdens of a different sort. He is trying to live in two worlds — the traditional Native world and the world of modern American culture.

It is not an easy task, for the two do not easily fit together. But when someone masters the challenge, it is a beauty to behold, because their life embraces the richness and promise of the American experience in a way that those of us from a single cultural experience can only dream of understanding.

The three of us are walking through the knee-high grasses toward a low rock outcropping that rises like the back of a humpback whale from the center of this windswept prairie.

Buffalo grasses, prairie flowers, and miles of gently undulating earth stretch in all directions to the horizon.

It is easy to imagine the creak of wooden wheels and the billowing tops of covered wagons moving across this landscape beneath azure blue skies alive with butterflies and tumbling cotton-ball clouds. It is a place of profound and infinite peace.

We have come here at Raymond's request. I had spoken to him of the petroglyphs — small symbols and forms scratched into acres of these low, barely visible humps of rock that rise from this quiet prairie landscape — and he had expressed a desire to see them.

No one knows quite why these petroglyphs are here or by whom they were made. Anthropologists and historians theorize, but can do little more than guess at the meanings of these thousands of markings. A snake form here, a stick figure there, the outline of a hand, a shape like the back of a turtle.

How many generations, even eons, did humans stop here, and for what purpose, to make these scratchings into unyielding stone? They are older than Stonehenge, older than the pyramids.

I stand transfixed, suspended between wonder and reverie, letting my thoughts flow across the undulating prairies, while Martin and Raymond walk together — father and son — among the glyphs and markings, speaking quietly to each other.

Soon I see Raymond get down on his knees and bend over, as if perhaps kissing the rock. Then Martin does the same.

I look more closely.

They are not kissing the rock. They are bringing out an abalone shell and a pouch of sage to make their own small offering to the spirits of the people who made these markings, and perhaps to the very stones themselves.

They are not trying to understand; they are honoring the presence and the mystery.

They invite me to join them. I kneel next to Raymond as Martin, at his father's instruction, lights the sage and begins an invocation to the forces that float like the butter-flies across this vast, peaceful land.

I follow their lead, opening my heart in prayerful awareness to the spirits that surround us.

It is not my world — I am too far separated from it by the overlays of my Euro-American upbringing and her-itage. But, by the gift of their invitation, I am allowed to enter into this world that stretches, in unbroken tradition, from the hands that had marked these stones to the hands that are cupping the smoke and shaping the sage on the hard rock before us.

When we are finished, we all remain silent in the echo-ing presence of this ancient ritual. Then, one by one, we wander off in our separate directions across the great rock outcroppings, lost in our own private thoughts. I see Martin and Raymond at a distance, silhouetted against the after-noon sky.

Below my feet I feel the presence of the great rock. Among the markings, barely visible, I see the outline of an ancient hand, scratched there tens of thousands of years ago by an unknown traveler. Without thinking, I get down and place my hand against the outline. It fits perfectly.

My hand is warm. The stone is cold. But in the touch something is passed, and I am humbled beyond under-standing.

·:·:·

Years ago I was talking with a Native man from northern Michigan who liked to speak to groups about his traditional Native ways. One of his favorite stories was about stones.

"How many of you," he would ask, "have ever walked along the beach and picked up a single stone?"

In all his years of asking thousands of people this question, only one had never had this experience. The rest, like me, had smiled and nodded their affirmation. Yes, we had picked up a stone, put it in our pocket, and taken it home, or had carried it for a while, turning it in our hand, and then tossed it far out into the lake or sea.

"Why," he asked, "did you choose that stone?"

No one had an answer.

"Because," he continued, "that stone called out to you. We don't pick up stones on the street or on a hillside. But the stones at the edge of the water — they have been carried there, have been left there. They have felt the motion of the water. They are hungry to move."

He went on to comment, in typically wry Native fashion, that these stones were tired of sitting where they were and wanted to go on a trip.

"So they call out to us," he said, "to pick them up, to take them home, or to throw them far out in the water. It's the first time they've gotten to move in thousands of years."

His manner was joking, but there was conviction at its core. Bred deep in his bones, bred deep in his Native heart, was the belief that there is spirit in everything in creation and that everything has a voice, if only we have the ears — or, in this case, the spirit — to hear.

I understood something of what he was saying.

For years I worked as a sculptor in wood, laboring with only a mallet and hand chisels, seeking to coax images from large tree trunks.

I would begin my carving with an idea and try to impose it on the tree. But at some point the tree would begin to speak back to me, asserting its own personality and presence and mocking the sufficiency of my own concept with the sheer force and power of its own character.

Some were strong and muscular, with the confidence of decades of unimpeded growth.

Others were quiet and yielding, reflecting a gentle life in gentle soils.

Still others had encountered difficult years or unsupportive terrain.

And all possessed the character of their particular species as well as a personality born of their particular life experience.

I remember once working on an oak tree that was so profoundly sad that I could hardly bear to carve on it. It was in the smell — a strange, sickly sweetness; in the feel — a spongy response to the chisel; and in the constant changes in density and texture. But those were only the external manifestations of a deep sadness that came from the very life force of the tree itself.

To deny that life force or to reduce it to objective characteristics like texture and scent was akin to saying that the life force in humans is the sum of our bones and blood and muscles. It ignores the sheer mysterious power that courses through us, animating those individual elements. There is something that brings all those disparate elements alive, putting light in our eyes and dreams in our hearts. It is a spiritual presence that courses through the rest of nature as well, and if it is impossible to describe and quantify, it is no less real for being so.

Those of us who live with dogs, cats, horses, or other animals have no difficulty understanding this. But we quickly come up against our limits when we move from those elements of creation to those that have no apparent consciousness.

This is what I was able to transcend, if only unwittingly, by my relationship with the trees I carved. They were individual, they were alive, and they spoke in voices, though not the kind of voices I had been raised to hear.

-:::-

Why was it that for untold generations, men and women stopped at these unassuming outcroppings of rock that rise only ever so slightly above the surrounding prairie, and scratched and etched crude images into the hard and nearly impenetrable stone?

Anthropologists can spend their time trying to ascertain the meaning of these symbols, and that is a worthy pursuit.

But is there not a larger question of why generations of people, separated from each other by time and culture, stopped here, exactly here, to create those symbols?

My friend in Michigan would say that it was because the stone called out to them, just as the stones that we pick up on the beach call out to us to be claimed and moved.

Is this so strange and poetic that we cannot give it credence?

From the human to the animal to the tree to the stone is not so great a leap if we open our hearts to the possibility of an inhering spiritual presence in all of creation. That we acknowledge this presence only in humans, with a small nod to the consciousness of animals, does not necessarily reflect truth more than it reflects limitation.

The Native people, even if they cannot now make the full journey back to the voices in the stones, at least do honor to the possibility.

Raymond and Martin, by their simple and timeless ceremony, were giving that honor. To perform a ceremony that has been done for thousands of years, even if it is done with diminished ritual knowledge, is to touch a power that defies understanding and to open one's spirit to a different level of awareness.

I do not know where Martin and Raymond went in their spirits as they knelt over their offerings, any more than I know the intentions of the people who knelt on this low rock outcropping thousands of years ago and scratched these images of snakes and thunderbirds and human hands into this unforgiving stone. I do not know how close they came, or how close any of us can come, to hearing the voices in the stones.

But I do know that, for a moment, standing in this lonely prairie with the wind blowing the grasses in their timeless dance, I was called to awareness by the ceremony those two good men performed, and in that moment I was tied to the earth, and to all those who have walked upon it, in a way as solid and fundamental as the very rock itself.

WIND AT THE BEAR'S PAW

Nature Is a Voice to Be Heard, Not a Force to Be Controlled

For after all the great religions have been preached and expounded... man is still confronted with the Great Mystery.

— LUTHER STANDING BEAR

THE WIND IS LOUD HERE. Strangely loud. Not loud like a roar, but like a strong and urgent whisper.

It is 4:30 A.M. The first hint of dawn is limning the horizon. I am lying in a small earthen depression on a low hilltop in the empty high plains of northern Montana, trying to apprehend something beyond my understanding.

To the casual passerby, this depression would go unnoticed. It is little more than a hollow in the ground, almost hidden by the thick prairie grasses that keen and rattle in the relentless high-plains wind.

But to those who know, this depression tells a story.

It was here, in October of 1877, that a ragged remnant

of the Nez Perce people, the most powerful tribe in the Northwest, finally gave up their eighteen-hundred-mile journey in a desperate attempt to escape to Canada, where they believed they would be free from the control of the U.S. government and able to live, raise their children, and care for their families in the ways that had been handed down to them by their ancestors.

This depression, now almost invisible in the whispering high-plains grasses, is what remains of a rifle pit dug with frenzied hands by the few remaining Nez Perce warriors as they tried in vain to form a barrier between the advancing U.S. soldiers and the women, the elderly, and the children huddled in the draws below.

It is a sad and lonely place, this Bear's Paw. It would be forgotten by all, were it not for the surrender speech spoken here by Chief Joseph when he rode across this frozen landscape, handed his rifle to the U.S. military commander, and spoke the now famous words, "From where the sun now stands, I will fight no more forever."

The reality is much more complex, but no less poignant. In this lonely place, four hundred men, women, and children — those who remained of the eight hundred who had begun the journey from their homeland on the border between Idaho and Oregon — had made a last campsite before pushing on the final forty miles to the safety of Canada. They had been traveling for over three months, pursued by the U.S. military through mountain passes, burning alkali deserts, and frigid high-plains blizzards.

Their horses were sick. Their shelters were gone. Their food supplies were almost depleted. Mothers, fathers, sons, and daughters had perished during the journey and been buried in makeshift graves along the side of the trail.

Of those who remained, all had lost loved ones, and all believed that they would never see their homeland again.

With weary bodies and heavy hearts, they had made this one last stop to allow the sick and elderly to gather their strength for the final push through the early winter winds and snows to the safety of Canada, only a day's journey away.

What they did not know as they huddled in these hollows was that a new, well-provisioned U.S. army — the seventh that had been sent against them — was following the smoke from their campfires and quietly moving into position on the surrounding hills.

On a cold morning, with the snow line descending low on the distant mountains and ice forming on the creeks, these soldiers, with the aid of friendly Indians who had been conscripted to assist in the capture, burst down from these hills, scattering the Nez Perce camp, stampeding their few remaining horses, and sending the people running in terror for any sort of shelter or sanctuary they could find.

A few of the hearty were able to escape. But those who

were too weak or exhausted, or who chose not to abandon their ailing and wounded children and elders, huddled in hastily dug shelter pits while the soldiers lay siege to them, lobbing cannon shells from the promontories and slowly starving them into submission.

After six days, they could endure no more. Freezing, terrified, near starvation, with the children crying and the grandmothers singing their death songs, they came forth, one by one, and gave themselves up to a government that had vowed to use every power at its command to annihilate them and their way of life.

-:::-

I look around me at the empty hills stretching to the horizon. There are ghosts here, ghosts far beyond my understanding.

I see them now, in my mind's eye, hobbling up these hills, their feet wrapped in rags, their children clutched to their breasts, the young helping the blind and elderly.

I see the soldiers, themselves young and frightened, staring in disbelief at the ragged collection of sick and elderly who had been able to evade the best that the U.S. army had to offer for over three months and almost two thousand miles.

I see them, and I am overwhelmed with sadness. I have

followed this journey for four long years in a quest to tell the story of these Nez Perce people, who are now all but lost to our nation's memory.

During those four years I have come to know them as friends — the woman who had to kill her baby to keep it from crying and giving away their location to the soldiers, the families who had to leave elderly grandparents singing their death songs on the side of the trail because they were too weak to go any farther, the little girl who broke free from her mother's grip and ran back to her family's make-shift teepee during a hail of bullets to get the doll she had left behind.

These have been my companions. These, and this relentless wind, alive with echoes and memories.

The Native people understand the wind. That is why they listen to it, why they have given it names and power and life.

It is why they will stop at a moment's notice to listen to its call, and why they will respect it as the bringer of messages from beyond the boundaries that bind us — time, space, the grave itself.

For them, the wind bears a truth too great to ignore. And they bow their heads before it.

I remember one January night when I was working on the Red Lake reservation. I was lying in my bed in our home in the northern Minnesota woods, listening to the wind howl and shake the rafters above me. I was bothered, afraid, unable to sleep. Something seemed wrong.

When I went to work on the reservation the next day, I mentioned it to the woman who prepared meals for the elders. She had been raised in the traditional way, and I often went to her for guidance and advice.

"That was an angry wind last night," I said.

She did not look up. "Yes," she said. "A baby died."

It was more than an answer; it was a lesson.

This is the Native world. There are no coincidences, no disconnected acts. Every gesture has meaning; every action has significance. A dark wind carries dark knowledge; a bright wind brings happiness and good fortune.

The elders seldom talk about this, and not with outsiders. It is too easily misinterpreted, too easily turned into a false and facile mysticism. And yet the knowledge is there. It is passed on to the children in a glance, a word, or a quiet remonstration. "Do not take things so lightly," it says. "Nothing is an accident; everything is connected."

It is this connection I am feeling as I lie here in this rifle pit with the frail light of dawn etching the edges of the surrounding hills.

The wind rushes past me, urgent, hissing, threatening. It feels like a mother bird, flying desperately over my head, trying to distract me from the nestlings to whom I have come too close.

I hear its voice, just as I saw the images of the frightened, hungry people just beyond the edges of my understanding. "Get out of here," it seems to say. "Get out of here. You do not belong here."

I listen to its frantic urgings, sensing in them both a pleading and a violence. They whisper of a darker truth — that I am on the edge of violating something fundamental, and that such violations do not go unnoticed in a realm that is far from my understanding.

Like a man in a graveyard, suddenly overcome with a nameless shudder, I feel the wrongness of my presence.

I rise from the hollow and hurry down the path from the battlefield toward the safety of the small ribbon of roadway half a mile away.

I cross the creek where Joseph and his people huddled and make my way through the hillocks where soldiers and young warriors died.

I feel a presence at my back; a fear overcomes me. I need to leave here. The wind is screaming at me, and I need to leave here.

Back in my car and its fragile illusion of protection, I look across the now lightening hills at the whispering grasses, rolling one way, then the other, as the wind bends them to its will.

I am humbled, chastened, and not a little bit afraid.

I turn the key, hear the comforting hum of the motor,

the familiar sequence of mechanical parts working in unison. Sealed in a small world of human devise, surrounded by the fruits of human creation, I feel safe and protected, once again in charge of my own life.

But just outside, the wind still blows, and the grasses do their ghostly dance. And I am reminded, once again, that the unseen is not the unreal, but only that which is beyond our understanding, and that the truth of life is not found in knowledge, but in something close to prayer.

EPILOGUE

The Shadow and the Vision

As I close this sketchbook of reflections gained from thirty years of living near to the heartbeat of Native America, I would like to leave you with a few thoughts about the Native people and our American experience.

From the beginning, we who came from other lands were ambivalent about the people we encountered when we first set foot upon these shores.

On one hand, we saw them as the innocents — the pure unsullied children of nature, untainted by the very wiles and snares of the civilization that we sought to escape when we left the confines of our European existence and set sail on a journey in search of freedom from religious, social, and economic restraints.

On the other, they were the dark force, the shining eyes at night in the forest, the primitive and threatening unknown bound by no rules of civil behavior — almost more animal than human.

In them we saw reflected the best and the worst of the human character — the savage and the innocent — and they rested uncomfortably in our national psyche. They were the embodiment of our greatest dreams and our greatest fears.

As we made our way through history, seeking the land we needed to build a civilization in accordance with our vision, we annihilated these people — by force, by fiat, by assimilation, by cultural genocide.

They were the barrier to the onward march of progress, the sad but inevitable collateral damage in the fulfillment of our destiny to subdue this continent and make it bear fruit. No act of violence or guile was beyond us in our effort to take their land and claim it as our own.

But beneath this thirst to advance our civilization, our ambivalence always remained.

We could destroy the First Peoples physically, but we could not erase their presence from our hearts.

And so we hid them, buried them deep in our cultural psyche, just as we had buried so many of them in the earth they once had called their own. They became the shadow of our cultural guilt.

But shadows do not cease to exist merely because we refuse to look at them.

The shadow of the Native peoples and all they represent remained, and it remains today. We have merely changed the language we use and the way we understand them.

The child of nature became the earth mother and

wisdom-bearing elder. The uncivilized savage became the drunk and the layabout.

Yet the real people — the good fathers and mothers and grandparents and families, doing their best to live worthy lives and raise healthy children with hearts full of hope — remain as well. But we do not choose to see them, because they hold up a mirror to our wanton destruction of a people and a way of life.

We want the images, not the reality. We do not wish to see the blood on the ground where we have walked.

But we do this at our own peril.

By ignoring the real people and their existence, we lose more than an honest understanding of a dark but significant part of our history. We lose a link to a rare expression of humanity — a way of living and being that, though now diminished by centuries of suppression and oppression, still contains within it, if sometimes only as a distant echo, the core of beliefs and humane ways that were born of deep experience of this American land.

It is a way where giving is the greatest human value, and our first responsibility is toward each other, not toward ourselves; where spirit is believed to be present in all things; where no person pushes his or her way of believing upon another; where family is all those you hold in your heart, and the children and elders are held sacred because they are closest to the Creator.

It is a way that understands limits and humility and forgiveness; that recognizes that all people need to feel needed and are best made to feel needed by being given roles appropriate to their talents.

It is a way that sees the past as a teacher and something to be honored, not something to be transcended.

Do the Native people always live up to these beliefs in their day-to-day lives?

Of course not. Who among us, as individuals or as a culture, always lives up to our highest vision of ourselves?

It is to the eternal credit of the Native peoples that they retain even the echoes of these beliefs and practices after five hundred years of concerted efforts to eradicate their way of life and their very presence on this earth.

But their vision still remains, and it guides them, as it could guide us all.

I often think of a comment made by John Oberly, the commissioner of Indian affairs in the late nineteenth century.

"The Indian," he said, "must be imbued with the exalting egotism of American civilization, so that he will say 'I' instead of 'We' and 'This is mine,' instead of 'This is ours.'"

Is this truly the way we wish to understand the world?

Is this truly the vision of who we want to be and what we wish to pass along to our children?

We Americans are caught in a web of our own creation. We celebrate the individual; we praise self-reliance.

We have built our entire economic system on competition and striving, where we set ourselves one against the other in the belief that if each of us pursues our own ends, the result will be a fostering of the common good.

Yet even those of us most committed to this vision recognize that there are limits to this celebration of the self. Our focus on the individual and "exalted egotism" now too often seems to subvert the common good it was meant to serve.

·:·

I am disinclined to end on a cautionary note. We Americans are a people of optimism and possibility and do not respond well to cautions and talk of limitations.

But the world exists independent of our understanding of it. It was here before we came into existence; it will be here long after we are gone. It operates by rules far different from ours and answers to forces far beyond our understanding and control.

I am reminded of the words of the elder who said:

Nature has rules. Nature has laws. You think you can ignore the rules or, if you don't like them, you can change them. But Mother Earth doesn't change the rules.

When you can count the animals, you're getting

near the end of your chances. We can count the eagles. We can count the buffalo. I've heard that in India and Africa they can count the tigers and the elephants. That's Mother Earth crying out. She's giving us a warning, and she's begging for her life.

And here's what your people don't ever seem to learn. There's going to come a day when things can't be fixed.

And you know what? It's going to be a day just like today.

We don't want that day to come, for ourselves or for our children, and we don't want that to be the legacy of our time on earth.

We want to leave this a better place, a more hopeful place, a more caring and humane place for our children and all the children who follow.

I firmly believe that the Native people have something to teach us in this regard. If we look past the dysfunction born of the cultural devastation that has been visited upon them, look beyond the guilt that has blinded us and the mythologies we have fostered; if we see past their small numbers and our tendency to dismiss them as just another minority group, we may yet come to realize that they are not a vanquished culture, they are our elder culture, and they have unique gifts to offer as the original children of this land.

·:::·

I would like to leave you with a simple story of a letter I received from a young Native friend of mine. He had traveled from his home in the Alaskan panhandle to the town of Barrow, one thousand miles farther north on the icy shores of the Arctic Ocean, where he was visiting with the Inupiaq people, one of the groups most of us know as Eskimos.

A good man and respectful of the ways of others, he had been granted the honor of being present at a whale hunt.

He was, quite naturally, awed and humbled by what he saw. Against the stark simplicity of this land of sea and ice, he was witness to an elemental meeting of species, an encounter that had its roots in the deepest cultural heritage of the Inupiaq people.

It was sustenance, it was survival, it was the meeting of life and death.

After watching the people labor together to pull the whale onto the ice, and seeing the meat be cut into chunks to be shared among all members of the community, he wrote me a note. This is what it said:

> Standing before a one-hundred-thousand-pound animal that was fifty-seven feet long and lying on the ice was a powerful feeling. The animal's spirit lingered in the air, and I could feel it.

I was saddened by her death. It was a she, and she had lived a long and prosperous life. I imagine she had decided it was her time.

She lived with pure thought and good intention full of delicate love. She dreamed once. She cried at one time and loved her young with the love that only a mother carries for her child.

She has encountered dangers in the past and persevered. She's felt emotion, as we have. If she could speak, imagine the stories she could tell.

I'd like to imagine she even gave thanks to the Creator, and I imagine she even prayed in her own primitive way, a way that is and was as beautiful as ours.

She gave her life to us. To the Great Spirit.

We give thanks. Saddened and proud, humbly and solemnly, we give thanks to the Creator and to her for this wonderful gift.

Is this not a worthy way to look at the world around us — with eyes of wonder and humility? To see the spirit in all things that live, to look upon all of life's bounty as a gift, and to honor the difficult task we have of being worthy stewards of this land?

How much better this seems than the idea of "exalted egotism," where we are taught to "say 'I' instead of 'We' and 'This is mine' instead of 'This is ours.'"

This is not to denigrate who we are. Our American tradition, too, has a genius well worth sharing.

Ever moving, ever changing, ever transforming and inventing, we are the people of limitless curiosity and endless possibility.

But in our celebration of our limitless potential, we have not paid heed to the land with its lessons and cautionary notes. Instead, we have sought to master it and transform it. We have not seen it as our teacher.

But the earth is teaching now, and demanding that we listen. She is saying that our idea of freedom has been too committed to the human, too tied to the self, too deaf to the voice of the rest of nature.

She is asking us to see that we are a part of nature, not apart from her, and to recognize the delicate interconnections that bind us all.

This way of understanding has been bred into the hearts of Native people, and it lives there today.

To listen to their voices is to learn how to watch, to pay attention, to understand and respect the interconnections.

It is to honor rather than master, to understand limits as well as to celebrate possibilities.

It is to hear the voice of nature before attempting to bend her to our will.

In short, it is to look upon our place on earth with

humility, and to bow our heads before the responsibility, as well as the possibilities, that this places before us.

The Shoshone elder whose words open this book may yet be right: perhaps we did come here to learn from the Native people.

But perhaps the truth lies even deeper.

Perhaps we came to meld our unique genius of restless curiosity and discovery with their unique genius of quiet attention to the spiritual in all the works of creation.

Perhaps, in a place and time beyond our knowing, there is a unity yet to be achieved.

Perhaps there is a meeting place for those who listen to the earth and those who set their sights beyond the stars.

But for now, here on the earth that we all share, the task is much simpler. It was stated most beautifully by the great Lakota chief Sitting Bull, when he spoke to the U.S. government that had committed to eradicating the ways of his people from this earth.

"Come," he said, "let us put our minds together to see what kind of lives we can create for our children."

Is there a worthier goal or more sacred task for any of us than this?

AUTHOR'S NOTE

THROUGHOUT THIS BOOK I quote extensively from traditional Native leaders, most notably Luther Standing Bear, Ohiyesa, and, to a lesser extent, Chief Joseph. I count these men as mentors and models and encourage all readers to seek out their writings.

Rather than give an extensive bibliography, I will only mention those works that I cite most frequently and that have been most influential in shaping my understanding.

Luther Standing Bear's thought is brilliantly revealed in *Land of the Spotted Eagle.*

Ohiyesa, or Charles Alexander Eastman, touched me most deeply in *The Soul of the Indian.*

Chief Joseph's mind and heart are best expressed in the poignant speech he gave in January of 1879 at Lincoln Hall in Washington, D.C.

All of these men's thoughts, as well as those of many other greathearted Native people, are collected in my work *Wisdom of the Native Americans* (New World Library, 1999). Chief Joseph's story is recounted in detail in my book *Chief*

Joseph and the Flight of the Nez Perce: The Untold Story of an American Tragedy (HarperOne, 2005).

I once wrote that Ohiyesa is a man to whom I would have entrusted my country or my son. The same is true for the other men as well. Those among us who are looking for a more civil and humane way to live would do well to heed the lessons of their words.

I also need to point out, on a personal note, that in many instances throughout the book I have changed the names of people whose stories I tell. Unless they expressly gave me permission to use their names, it seemed prudent and respectful to protect their identities. Some of the best people are also the most self-effacing and the least willing to be put forward as exemplars or models. I do not wish to violate their privacy simply to tell a story or make a point. But I believe their stories need to be told and the examples of their lives made known.

Finally, I should emphasize that not all Native cultures are the same, any more than all European nations are the same. I think that the values I have tried to bring forth are common throughout Native America, though reflected in different ways.

Pan-Indianism is a danger whenever speaking of Native America and, though time, cultural interpenetration, and the melting pot of the boarding-school experience have all served to bring the many Native peoples closer together in the modern world, the roots of their individual beliefs and cultures are unique and personal.

What is unequivocally universal is their belief that spirit permeates all of creation, and this has been my core conviction in trying to show you the ways that Native America has influenced my life and thought.

I hope you find these ways meaningful for your own life as well.

ABOUT THE AUTHOR

KENT NERBURN IS WIDELY RECOGNIZED as one of the few American writers who can respectfully bridge the gap between Native and non-Native cultures. Novelist Louise Erdrich has called his work "storytelling with a greatness of heart." Nerburn is the author or editor of fifteen books on spirituality and Native themes, including *Chief Joseph and the Flight of the Nez Perce*, *Simple Truths*, *Small Graces*, and *Letters to My Son*. The volumes in his groundbreaking trilogy, *Neither Wolf nor Dog: On Forgotten Roads with an Indian Elder*, *The Wolf at Twilight: An Indian Elder's Journey through a Land of Ghosts and Shadows*, and *The Girl Who Sang to the Buffalo: A Child, an Elder, and the Light from an Ancient Sky*, are considered core works in the multicultural curriculum of schools and colleges around the world. After twenty-five years in the rugged lake country of northwestern Minnesota, he and his wife, Louise Mengelkoch, have moved to the cedar-scented richness of the Pacific Northwest with their elderly yellow Lab, Lucie. His website can be found at www.kentnerburn.com.

NEW WORLD LIBRARY is dedicated to publishing books and other media that inspire and challenge us to improve the quality of our lives and the world.

We are a socially and environmentally aware company. We recognize that we have an ethical responsibility to our customers, our staff members, and our planet.

We serve our customers by creating the finest publications possible on personal growth, creativity, spirituality, wellness, and other areas of emerging importance. We serve New World Library employees with generous benefits, significant profit sharing, and constant encouragement to pursue their most expansive dreams.

As a member of the Green Press Initiative, we print an increasing number of books with soy-based ink on 100 percent postconsumer-waste recycled paper. Also, we power our offices with solar energy and contribute to non-profit organizations working to make the world a better place for us all.

Our products are available in bookstores everywhere.

www.newworldlibrary.com

At NewWorldLibrary.com you can download our catalog,
subscribe to our e-newsletter, read our blog,
and link to authors' websites, videos, and podcasts.

Find us on Facebook, follow us on Twitter, and watch us on YouTube.

Send your questions and comments our way!
You make it possible for us to do what we love to do.

Phone: 415-884-2100 or 800-972-6657
Catalog requests: Ext. 10 | Orders: Ext. 10 | Fax: 415-884-2199
escort@newworldlibrary.com

NEW WORLD LIBRARY
publishing books that change lives   14 Pamaron Way, Novato, CA 94949